WHY HAVEN'T YOU READ THIS BOOK?

Flipping the burden of proof to open
up a world of possibility

Edited by Isaac Morehouse

RIB??

Special thanks to Sheldon Richman for edits and comments on this book, Tim Meissner for his work making it look beautiful, and James Walpole for providing a fresh set of eyes.

CONTENTS

Introduction
Why haven't you flipped the burden of proof? *Isaac Morehouse*   9

Why haven't you dropped out of school? *Zachary Slayback*   15

Why haven't you moved to a new city? *Ben and Nicole Angelo*   41

Why haven't you written a book? *Jeffrey Tucker*   53

Why haven't you quit your job? *Peter Neiger*   61

Why haven't you started a business? *Levi Morehouse*   69

Why haven't you traveled the world? *Courtney Derr*   83

Why haven't you auditioned for American Idol? *TK Coleman*   97

Why haven't you had a bunch of kids? *Antony Davies*   109

Why haven't you flown first class? *Tim Chermak*   125

Why haven't you climbed a mountain? *Bob Ewing*   139

Conclusion
Why haven't you started yet? *Isaac Morehouse*   155

Introduction

Why haven't you flipped the burden of proof?

Isaac Morehouse

Introduction

All the best decisions in my life have come as a surprise to those around me. Met with a bewildered "why?" I used to feel the need to give lengthy justifications. Doing things out of the ordinary better have a good list of reasons, right? At some point I got tired of justifying myself and turned the question around. My response to "why?" became "Why not?" I felt a freedom I'd never experienced. It was a revolution.

My wife and I moved away from our hometown to a new city with few friends or family connections. Then we did it again -- to a city with even fewer. We had a few compelling reasons and mostly a burning question. Why not? More than once I've quit an excellent job I loved in order to do something quite a bit different. It seemed weird to my colleagues, but the opportunity to take a dramatic turn on my life path had no compelling arguments against it. Then I started a business, even though I hate a lot of the businessy stuff it requires. I had an idea that was interesting, so why not?

I have not (yet) climbed a mountain or auditioned for *American Idol*, and I doubt you'd count our three kids as "a bunch," but we are embarking on some extended world travels and generally attempting to implement the ideas that animate the book you are now reading. This doesn't make me special or give you reason to take my word, but I hope it illustrates that this book is about a way of life I've found great personal fulfillment in.

What this book is about

This book is about the simple practice of flipping the burden of proof from "why" to "why not." What would happen to your life if you stopped assuming you know all the reasons why not to do things differently? Have you ever really, seriously demanded of yourself good reasons to *not* start a business, move to a new city, drop out of school, quit your job, write a book, travel the world, climb a mountain, fly first class, audition for *American Idol*, or have a bunch of kids?

You probably assume you have good reasons for not doing these things. We all do. It's called status quo bias. The dominant path isn't scrutinized much, while deviations are. That's the line anyway. We think the deviations are scrutinized, but maybe they're scrutinized even less. Over time we assume other people have already asked questions and demanded answers of alternative choices. There must be a reason people largely make the same big decisions, right? Society is onto something, right?

The default is to believe you don't need to give a reason for not taking a big risk and being different. We just kind of know it's a bad idea. But do we really know?

What this book is not about

The point of this book is not to argue in favor of any of the big ideas put forth. It's not to argue against the status quo either. It's to challenge you to be a better questioner when it comes to your own life choices. You don't have to do any of the things discussed in these pages. But before you say no to them, demand good, honest reasons why you shouldn't.

Consider all the life-altering choices that don't get much scrutiny. Buying a home, going to college, getting a typical 9-5, and so on. Is that what you want? Are you sure? Would your life look different if you asked "why?" of all the things that don't get questioned, and "why not?" of all those that do?

If not, good for you. Now when you settle into your path you'll at least know you consciously chose it and you'll know why. This is a big help when times get tough. On the other hand, if in flipping the burden of proof you find better reasons to do something previously thought out of reach or radical, good for you too. You've done the hard work of knowing thyself. The harder work of acting on it comes next!

It is my belief that the best decisions are fun, challenging, and not tainted with guilt, obligation, shame, or fear. Don't read this book and feel like you have to do something different to be cool. If it's not you and you have plenty of sound "why nots," don't do it. Just have reasons. Your reasons, not anyone else's.

Status quo bias exists for a reason. It's a good thing we don't have to rediscover all pitfalls and dangers firsthand. "Why not touch the hot stove?" is probably a bad example of flipping the burden of proof. The reason this contrarian approach is valuable is precisely because it's only valuable sometimes for some people in some situations. We can't tell you all the best times to apply it, but a little common sense should go a long way. Test it out in your head before you take action. I bet you can answer "Why not touch the hot stove" without touching it first.

You don't need to eschew all traditions and norms and common advice. They're helpful more often than not. But at least find out why they're helpful and whether they apply to you in every situation. The big breakthroughs happen when you find exceptions to rules, but you'll never find them if you only ask the same questions everyone else is asking.

Why should you trust the authors?

Of course I'm going to respond, "why not?" None of the authors are experts. Instead, this book is a collection of ideas and stories from people who have lived these out-of-the-norm decisions, sometimes with wonderful results, sometimes with great difficulty. The authors were chosen primarily because I love their stories and outlook, and also because they are all friends of mine whom I find fascinating and inspirational.

This book is very down to earth. Each chapter is done in the style and tone of its author, and I made no great effort to unite them with a single voice. Some read as tips and how-to's, some read as personal stories. But the authors have each put their lives where their words are and asked "why not?" of some big, crazy decisions. You can read the chapters in any order you like -- skip around to the topics most intriguing.

I gave the authors free reign when I invited them to contribute to this book. You'll find great variation in length, depth, and breadth of the chapters. I didn't want to force people into arbitrary length, even if it made the table of contents more uniform. Sorry if that bugs you.

This collection is just a sampling of things most people assume are bad ideas but that might turn out to include the best thing for you if you flip the burden of proof and examine it closely. There are infinite possible applications of this practice. You'll have to think for yourself to discover your own "why nots."

01.

Chapter One

Why Haven't You Dropped Out of School?

Zak Slayback

I had near-perfect grades through high school, attended my first-choice school -- an Ivy League university -- on a scholarship, worked on a prestigious summer research fellowship, and, had I chosen that route, had the stars aligning to attend a top-tier graduate school. I was far from struggling in my classes -- I had even designed the syllabus with a professor for a majors-only seminar I participated in and went on to take a graduate seminar as a sophomore. I was active on campus, participating in and leading several clubs.

In brief, I was an ideal college student.

Two years in and I dropped out. And this started with asking myself, "Why haven't I dropped out of college?"

A quick disclaimer

Before getting into my personal story of leaving school, I want to note that *I love learning*. Most discussions over the relative value of staying in versus leaving school focus on whether somebody truly values learning. Advocates of the latter allow themselves to be painted as anti-intellectuals, people opposed to the liberal arts, hyper-practical handymen just concerned with what will be marketable in the future. Get rid of that idea right now. Learning and schooling are not the same thing. Sometimes the best learning takes place in school, but that's increasingly not the case when opportunity costs are taken into account. Even more, classroom learning and schooling don't have to be the same thing. You can drop out of college and still enjoy classroom learning. (In fact, you can get the learning for free by auditing classes.)

If you love learning but aren't crazy about school, this chapter is for you.

College over high school

I enrolled in college, initially, because I wanted to build things. This didn't necessarily mean pursuing a STEM (science-technology-engineering-math) track -- I just enjoyed the process of building, whether simple Legos as a child or organizations and idea-systems as a young adult. College was a step up from rigid high school and appeared to be a prerequisite for any kind of building I wanted to do.

Restless and anxious as a student of the No Child Left Behind-era in public schools, I wondered why we were spending so much time sitting in assemblies about the PSSA (Pennsylvania System of School Assessment) tests and how to properly answer multiple-choice questions when that had no bearing on what I wanted to learn about. Why were we focusing on some ridiculous state-enforced standards that the teachers themselves admitted were totally arbitrary? Why did we take several *weeks* per year to do these exams? Why were the classes I enjoyed getting cut back for the ones that were enforced through testing regimens? High school became little more than jumping through hoops for state administrators.

School took me away from the learning I *wanted* to engage in and made me focus on things I didn't want. I loved learning; I just hated school.

I funneled this restlessness and anxiety into a drive to get into college. "I can focus on what I want to learn at college," I told myself. "Once I'm there, I can really get into the weeds of everything I need to know to go out and build what I want to do."

I was mostly wrong.

Once in college the anxiety moved from that which was enforced by anxious school administrators trying to please state education bureaucrats to something less-formally enforced but perhaps more oppressive.

Everybody says that your freshman year is *supposed* to be uncomfortable. You're *supposed* to struggle a little trying to find your place at the university, trying to figure out what you *really* want to do (because, you are told, your major will change several times, so it's silly to be sure of what you want) and who you *really* are. Your restless desire for definiteness of place and purpose at school will go away, you're assured. (Though this isn't said explicitly, many college students feel this -- that is why they join fraternities, sororities, and clubs at school, and study abroad.) The restlessness from high school wasn't gone, but I just figured it would go away after the first year.

It didn't.

Competition quashes progress

Perhaps more alarming was what was happening to my classmates. Many were peers I had met through various activities in high school and who were, at the time, some of the most interesting people I knew. They told me about how they wanted to be entrepreneurs, poets, artists, authors, engineers, and more. They, like me, were going to school as a means to achieving that life for themselves. Still others were generally impressive people who could have achieved anything to which they had fully committed themselves.

These classmates, many of whom had gotten into college with their unique and varied accomplishments, became obsessed with competition, with one-upping each other so they could get the top-tier job or get into the top-tier graduate school. At first glance this should be no surprise, right? *Of course* students at a top tier school would be competitive. That's what got them in in the first place, right?

Competition isn't an inherently good thing, especially on the individual level. [1] The cult of competition tells us that we have to focus on one-upping each other for a limited set of laurels. At my college it was competition over either pre-professional tracks or graduate-school tracks. Everybody wanted to land the internship with Goldman Sachs or Merrill Lynch. Everybody needed to get the perfect GPA so that he could get into the best medical school. A student at another top-tier school told me that students in her classes would compete to keep their GPAs high so that they could go to "first-page" law schools (meaning, law schools that were on the first page of the US *News and World Report* rankings).

Competition can be a good motivator if you know *why* you are engaging in it. If you aren't entirely sure why you are competing, or if your competing is entirely status-driven (as it is at the collegiate level), then competition actually quashes your ability to make personal progress.

To make personal progress you must first focus on what you want to achieve and build plans on how to carry this out. The competitive mindset is the antithesis of this. The difference between the personal mindset and the competitive mindset is where the locus of change sits. In the personal mindset the locus of change is with the individual. If John wants to achieve X, then he must compare himself against what it takes to achieve X and make the proper plans to get there. In the competitive mindset the locus of change is with other people. If John wants to achieve high status at his prestigious university, then he must beat out everybody else. So his plans are determined by what everybody is attempting to achieve.

The great paradox of status-driven competition is that everybody's focus is on everybody else. To get the most out of an elite degree you have to do the most with it. Doing the most with it demands that you do as much as have some of the most high-status people who attended the school while not falling behind your peers, who are going for the same thing.

Colleges and universities are breeding grounds for this counter-progressive competitive mindset. By organizing people into peer-groups (graduation classes, schools, majors), schools encourage comparison between students and between achievements. With GPAs determining awards like *magna cum laude* and admission to prestigious honor societies, college fosters a mindset in which everybody's success is governed by the actions of others.

I saw this mindset capturing my friends and peers. I began to see it creep into my own habits.

"This wasn't how it was *supposed* to be," I recall telling myself one day. I went to school to escape the competitive mindset of high school. I came here to gain the ability to go out and create the projects I wanted to create. I didn't come here to write papers that could be turned into writing samples for graduate school or entered into competitions with classmates for awards that look great on a resume or that impress a recruiter.

Just push through it?

As my sophomore year took off I knew I had to pour my restlessness into something *apart* from school to prevent falling into this trap. A friend of mine was launching a startup whose mission resonated with me.[2] I asked if I could pick up some extra work. He wouldn't have to pay me; I would do the work in my free time. It would allow me to pour out my energy without giving in to the temptation to spend that energy competing for top graduate-school slots or places on Wall Street.

The ability to really work on building something outside of an academic context was refreshing, to the point of nearly being a new experience entirely. Like many students, I had spent the last several years putting nearly all my efforts into something related to school. Classes in high school were curated to impress a college-admissions officer. Extracurriculars were a cross-section of what I enjoyed *and* what would help me with admissions. For the first time in years, I was able to do what I had been working toward this entire time: build something outside of school.

After my sophomore year I was presented with a challenge: I could either finish out my next two years of school while working on the startup and my other goals on the side, or I could go all-in on one or the other. I opted to take a year off and focus on building the startup while pursuing my education myself.

Trying to balance school and a startup would only end in mediocrity. You can't drive a new, radical idea like a startup (especially the kind on which we were working) with your efforts divided, aiming at two different futures. You can't get the most out of your limited and expensive college education by focusing most of your time elsewhere. Trying to juggle both produces mediocre results compared to going all-in on one or the other.

After continuing my work for several months, I was forced to ask myself why I was even in college in the first place. I told myself I had gone so that I could have access to the resources necessary to build projects. But here I was building a project.

I told myself that's what you need to do to get a job. But here I was with a (good) job.

I told myself that's what you need to do to take full advantage of your education. But here I was getting a better education than when I was enrolled as a full-time student.

I told myself that's what you need to do if you want a strong professional network. But here I was with a Rolodex worth more than the entire endowment of the university.

I told myself that's what you do to discover what you want to do. But I knew what I wanted to do since I was a young child, and school just obfuscated that for me.

So I dropped out.

What's the top idea in your mind?

Probably the best part about dropping out was the mental energy that it freed up. Before I dropped out, I told myself I had taken time off to focus on the startup and other projects full-time, but my mind was still ultimately governed by school -- or the eventual need to return.

Y Combinator co-founder Paul Graham has an essay called "The Top Idea in Your Mind."[3] This is essentially the idea that governs most of your actions. The moment of clarity you have in the shower in the morning, Graham says, is an example of the top idea in your mind.

When you are trying to balance school and an out-of-school project, your project cannot be the top idea in your mind. When school is almost inevitably governed by competition, your own progress cannot be the top idea in your mind. If everything you are doing while on leave or on your gap year is predicated on the belief that you will be returning to school, it cannot receive the benefit of your full attention.

Lots of college students try to launch startups while at school. Some even succeed. But your focus shouldn't be on whether your startup or project is successful for school purposes; rather, it should be on whether it is the best it can be. If you are just running it to pad your resume or to make your time at school seem more impressive, then you are running it for the wrong reasons and should just devote yourself fully to your studies.

(For this reason, I am skeptical of the obsession elite college students have with founding startups. It seems to be another indicator of a growing competitive mindset -- seeping from the university into the startup world, one that has traditionally been defined by a contrarian streak.)

If you want your own personal progress or the progress of your startup or project to be the top idea in your mind, you'll have a very hard time being on leave from school. You'd be best served by dropping out.

So why haven't you dropped out of college?

I recount my personal story because it *isn't* a story of somebody who struggled with school or who went in with a multimillion-dollar idea already rolling. I recount it because I have met hundreds of students in the past

several years who feel the same way I did -- anxious, restless, their purpose obfuscated by school -- and because I want to defend the idea that unless you have a very compelling reason to be in college, you are best served by dropping out.
Why do most people go to college?

Middle-class mimetics[4]

Before getting into specific reasons, to understand why most people (i.e., middle- and working-class people) say you should go to college in the United States today, we have to first understand the history of college education and the desire to "be successful."

The idea of achieving success in the United States has, over the last century or so, focused on some conception of "the American Dream." While the stereotype is two-and-a-half kids and a picket fence, as Americans started moving to the suburbs it generally became a struggle for the middle class and the working class to move into the upper-middle class. Those engaged in this struggle found hope in attending college and universities. Spurred by the the postwar GI bill, pundits and politicians alike propagated the belief that a university education would lead individuals and families to prosperity. The successful of the day were likely to have had college educations, making it appear as if a college education was a milestone on the path to success and stability.

All the while, as more people went to college and then into the workforce, the postwar economy started to pick up, not slowing down until the 1973 oil crisis. Baby-boomers grew up during the greatest expansion of the U.S. economy since the Gilded Age, then after many of them got out of college (and after the 1970s disruption), they saw the economic picture brighten once more in the 1980s and 1990s during the Reagan and Clinton eras (culminating in the dot-com bubble of 2001).

The idea that more higher education meant more success was intuitive enough for the boomers. They saw what those above economically them had, and they saw a strong correlation between higher education and economic growth during their lifetimes.

But this gets the process wrong on both counts.

Universities and colleges weren't *causes* of aristocracy and wealth; rather, they were *products* of aristocracy and wealth. Aristocrats didn't send their children to universities to make sure they got the tools necessary to stay aristocrats -- they sent them because it was essentially several years of leisure and only the most well-off could afford such a lifestyle.

The university was never intended to train people for high-wage jobs or to lift them up the economic ladder. At best it was an institution to train the clergy in the Middle Ages and then academics in the industrial age. This is why liberal-arts schools place such heavy emphasis on academic subjects -- they were designed to create professors.

As global wealth increased through the Industrial Revolution, aristocrats who were already comfortable in their wealth had two options for their children who were coming of age: A) send them to work, or B) give them some leisure among their same class. The university evolved into an institution to help young aristocratic men to transition into adulthood by moving away from home and studying subjects only the most well-off had the leisure to study. The backgrounds of elite American universities make this obvious. Princeton has "eating clubs"; Penn has "the Philomathean society"; and Yale's secret-society culture is a relic of this era.

This isn't a conspiracy. It's simply saying that the universities were never intended or designed for the use to which Americans of the mid-20th century put them. Agricultural schools of the antebellum era did start training people in practical trades, but even their growth was ill-suited to preparing people to create value in order to climb the economic ladder.

The postwar boom that the baby-boomers experienced in their youth was also not a product of a more-educated workforce. Immense technological growth from World War II, the rise of the semiconductor and information theory, and artificial growth stimulated by the Marshall Plan in Europe and American efforts to rebuild Japan were more likely causes of this long- and short-term growth. In other words, the gears of economic progress were in motion long before the boomers were even born, let alone before they attended school. PayPal co-founder Peter Thiel notes in *Zero to One*:

> Whether you were born in 1945 or 1950 or 1955, things got better every year of the first 18 years of your life, *and it had nothing to do with you.* Technological advance seemed to accelerate automatically,

so the Boomers grew up with great expectations but few specific plans for how to fulfill them.... Since tracked careers worked for them, they can't imagine they won't work for their kids, too.[5]

The myth that more formal schooling means more success is exactly that -- a myth. The United States is a culture that has been built by those who didn't wait for four years before taking on life: Thomas Edison, Cornelius Vanderbilt, Andrew Carnegie, John D. Rockefeller, Henry Ford, Mark Twain, Frank Lloyd Wright, Howard Hughes, Buckminster Fuller, Larry Ellison, Bill Gates, Steve Jobs, James Cameron, Travis Kalanick, Mark Zuckerberg, Harrison Ford are just a few examples.

That smarter people, on average, tend to go to college today, or that people with higher pay, on average, went to college can be explained by a simple selection bias. The cultural mythos we build around college propels smarter people and those more likely to achieve high pay in life (these are not always the same thing) along this path. They likely would have been successful without college.

With names like those above, why don't you start asking yourself, "Why haven't I dropped out of school?"?

A disclaimer: don't be Cheetos-Dude

Before looking at the reasons that might be holding you back from dropping out of college, I want to issue a quick disclaimer: dropping out of school is traditionally maligned because the alternative in most people's minds is to become "Cheetos-Dude." We all know Cheetos-Dude. He's the slacker who sits at home eating junk food and watching television when he has work to do. He's the guy who dropped out of college because it was too hard for him. He has a dead-end job because he's not willing to put in the work he needs to get a better job.

If you want to be Cheetos-Dude, by all means go ahead. This chapter isn't for you, though.

If you want to be more than Cheetos-Dude -- if you feel like you see Cheetos-Dude all over your college campus, like you've been cheated by the college mythos, like you might be able to do more with the freest years of your life -- keep reading.

The best way to prove a stereotype wrong is to live differently.

"I'm not like those you named."

Naming industrial titans, famous actors, and the men who built Silicon Valley isn't entirely fair, and it is exactly what the culture that glorifies college propagates. Like only those rare geniuses can go without. Maybe you thought about dropping out of college, but thought to yourself, "Yeah, but I'm not Steve Jobs or Mark Zuckerberg," or you had a family friend tell you, "Yeah, it made sense for *them*, but you aren't them!"

Get that idea out of your mind entirely. It's absurd, unfair, and not constructive.

At it's core this is a double standard. It's a double standard that tells college dropouts, "You won't be successful unless you reach the status of the mega-successful." Even more egregiously, it tells them, "If you aren't successful, you have nobody else to blame but yourself because you decided to drop out of college." It overlooks everybody else who didn't go to college and are moderately successful (and also forces somebody else's definition of success on you, but that's another topic entirely). It overlooks the college dropout who is just as successful as the banker down the street, the engineer next door, or the teacher one block over.

Nobody tells the college graduate, "You better be as successful as [the president of the United States, the chairman of Goldman Sachs, the CFO of Deloitte]! If you aren't as successful as [arbitrary standard I choose], then you have nobody else to blame but yourself because you decided to go to college!"

You don't need to be a Steve Jobs or a Mark Zuckerberg or a Harrison Ford to drop out of school. You don't need to abide by the double standard of the mythos built up and enforced by the boomers against their children. For every not-Steve Jobs or not-Mark Zuckerberg, there are dozens of not-Barack Obamas or not-Larry Pages. Next time you are hit with this justification for not dropping out, just flip the script.[6]

Chapter One

"I need a job."

If you ask most people why they went to college (and they are honest with you), they will likely tell you that it was so they could get a job. They didn't necessarily know what job or even what kind of job they wanted, but they just knew that they should go to college if they wanted to get a job.

This is absurd -- although not entirely their fault, considering how much teachers, parents, and guidance counselors probably pushed the "you need a degree if you want a decent job" dogma on them.

Going to college to study an indefinite field to get an indefinite job for an indefinite future sets the building blocks for an indefinite life. In other words, going to college without knowing what you want to get out of it or what kind of job you want to land just sets you up for not being in the driver's seat of your own life.

If you are sure of what you want to do and absolutely need a degree to do it (which pretty much just leaves lawyers, doctors, and academics), then go for it. But if you aren't sure, going "just because" sets a dangerous precedent for your own life.

That might sound like high-level abstract talk, but the idea that you go to college to get a job is absurd on the ground-level, too.

Employers who require college degrees don't do it because they necessarily think that those with college degrees are more likely to be valuable employees. Instead, this hiring practice is a relic of the pre-Internet era. It's an HR-move that helps companies sort out applications that are more or less likely to be worth looking at. If you were hiring in 1990, when college graduates were much fewer and when there was really no other way to verify a candidate's basic abilities like writing and showing up to work, a degree might have told you much more.

If you're hiring in 2015, when degrees are a dime-a-dozen and when Google is at your fingertips, college tells you considerably less about a candidate. It doesn't do a great job of sorting high-value candidates from low-value candidates when Jack, who showed up to class twice-per-semester and was always hungover, has the same BA as Sally, who showed up every day and never went out during school.

Richard Bolles's perennial bestseller, *What Color Is Your Parachute?*, goes through the basic steps for getting hired in a changing economy. Recent editions have included a chapter called "Google Is Your New Resume." What Bolles gets at here isn't that you need to be careful with what you post on social media (although you should), but rather that your entire portfolio of work is now available with a simple Google search of your name. If you want to be known as a designer, you can put up a site showing off your design work. If you have done sales, you can upload your sales decks to Slideshare. If you want to show off all your work generally, LinkedIn is the fastest-growing professional network in the world.

"Yeah, but lots of companies require BAs to get hired."

The BA requirement just shows that a candidate is a minimally viable candidate. It doesn't say anything else. A strong set of work experiences or a record of having created value in the marketplaces shows more than a BA does.

Many employers are changing their hiring copy slightly in light of degree-inflation. "BA or equivalent work experience" has started appearing on the websites of those who do require BAs. CEOs and hiring managers tell me this is because they realize the degree doesn't teach more than what some time in the field can teach.

Even more, degree requirements are disappearing entirely for companies born in the digital era or those trying to keep up with digital-era companies. Uber -- founded by UCLA dropout Travis Kalanick -- is a $51 billion company (at time of writing) that employs full-time business people, customer experience agents, and software engineers on every continent. Uber does not require a degree for many of their business positions.

"Okay, well, I'm going to figure out what I like and want."

Going to college to "discover yourself" or to "figure out what you want from life" are common reasons given by those who want to encourage more young people to attend. This overlooks a few facts:

    1) This is a very expensive way to figure out what you want.
    2) This is a very time-consuming way to figure out what you want.
    3) This isn't a very good way of figuring out what you want.

College is expensive. Everybody knows this. I don't have to type out the statistics on the average cost of a four-year undergraduate education here because it has been repeated so often it is almost cliche. It's easy to say "College is a great way to discover yourself!" when you aren't footing the bill.

And even if you don't have to pay a hefty price tag for four years of college experience, it's still four years of your life. The opportunity cost of college -- or the cost of all those activities that are forgone by spending your time in college -- is mind-bogglingly high. Recall the "equivalent work experience" requirement from above. That, if not more, is the opportunity cost of college.

Bill Gates returned to Harvard for a semester after launching Microsoft. If he had stayed in school instead of going back to Microsoft, his opportunity cost would have been the creation of all the wealth and value his tenure at Microsoft produced, and he would probably be considerably worse off for it.

Finally, the idea that college is a good place to figure out what you want is deeply flawed because it is an environment and institution almost entirely isolated from the real world, without real consequences for failure or success, and without real incentives (i.e., prices, profit, loss) influencing it.

To get an accurate picture of what you want from life (i.e., the time you spend in the "real world), you are best served by spending time in the real world. If you are like I was and are coming out of 12 years of compulsory schooling, you probably don't have a good idea of what the real world is like. Your past decade-plus has revolved entirely around school and what comes after school.

The best argument I've heard for using college to figure out what you want is that it provides a safe environment for you to try out different things and fail at them. If you fail and fall, you won't fall that far and you can get right back up and try something else, the argument goes.

But even this defense assumes too much of college. For many students, failure at school is tantamount to failure at life. Even those with a strong individualistic streak find themselves comparing their relative success in school to that of their classmates. They identify their success in life with their success as a student.

Failing at something in the real world isn't entirely bad, either. Most successful entrepreneurs fail at several ventures before they succeed. Most successful artists are rejected many times over before they get their break. Experiencing failure in the real world (and not the sanitized version of it found in college) might be good for many people, so long as they have the resolve to rebound from it. Attempting to avoid failure also puts a creative strain on the individual and provides an incentive to create and innovate in ways that would be difficult without this incentive.[7]

"I want higher pay."

"Studies show that going to college increases lifetime earnings by $1,000,000!"

You've likely heard this line repeated by pundits or high school guidance counselors. The message is clear: if you want higher pay, go to college.

But these kinds of studies are subject to a very strong selection bias.

The type of person who was more likely to attend college in 1990, 1995, or 2000 (the earliest time frames you could use for projecting lifetime earnings) is probably somebody who was moderately middle class, moderately intelligent, and moderately competent, at least. This person is then compared with the average student in the same age range who decided not to go to college – a less-impressive individual. The first person would have likely succeeded whether or not he went to school!

For a full analysis of earnings in light of schooling, researchers would have to follow twins from birth, making sure they had the same IQ and competence when they graduated high school. In other words, they would have to control for every variable influencing the individual's decision to go to college. No such study has been done.

The same kind of statistical logic can be used to justify going to an elite college over an average college, except here the poor logic has been hit with counter-studies.[8] Turns out that people who attend elite universities aren't necessarily going to earn more than their peers at average universities *because earnings are more than a reflection of education status.*

Recall what I said about the degree being a sorting mechanism for hiring. At one time this was also the case for giving raises, especially at the executive level. Getting an MBA would always be justified because it would bring a raise. As more people get MBAs and as more ways of comparing candidates arise, this is no longer the case. What was once considered a no-brainer is now highly contentious. What has happened to the MBA is an omen for what is going to happen (and is starting to happen) to the BA.

"I need a network."

College is said to be one of the best places to develop a network and get to know people who can be professionally helpful later in life. Whether it's a fraternity brother with business connections you can call on for your job-seeking son or a classmate that you decide to co-found a business with, colleges have traditionally been hubs of networking gold.

But is it the best place to acquire a network?

As a young person the most valuable kind of network you can acquire is one that is *vertically diverse*. This is a social network with lots of different people who are at more advanced stages of their careers than you. These are people who have built up social capital and are willing to go to bat for you when you most need somebody to go to bat for you. These are people with reputations and connections who are willing to listen to you. They're how you will most likely get your first job or two and how you will propel yourself forward. They're the ones who can connect you with VIPs (e.g., celebrities, investors, potential mentors).

The best way to actually acquire a vertically diverse network is to go out and work somewhere. Working at a high-growth startup is one of the best ways of doing this because it is high-risk and high-reward. If the startup succeeds, you gain the connections and laurels of being on a successful team. If it fails, you have at least gained the professional connections of those who joined you.

College provides you with lots of people at the same stage of life as you, although they might have different interests and backgrounds. As you get older, you will likely diverge a little, but not terribly. You'll stay in the general professional range as most of your peers. Your strongest connections will be with those in your immediate social circle, then your major, your school, your university, and your interests (e.g., sports, competitive clubs, etc.), in descending order. You may meet a few alumni, and you'll know some professors, but they'll be outside your field and won't be of much help to you after you graduate unless you pursue a career in academia.

A horizontally diverse network can be useful, for sure -- the PayPal mafia primarily went to two different schools and were almost all in the same age range -- but it isn't as powerful as a vertically diverse network for early professional life.

The best way to acquire a powerful professional network is to put some skin in the game and go out into the professional world.

"I need social interaction."

"The college experience" has become synonymous with everything from branching out into new social circles to reenacting *Animal House* every other weekend. Despite what liberal-arts professors will declare every year in articles at *Inside Higher Ed* and the *Huffington Post,* college is, for many students, a consumption good. They're looking to get a certain experience out of college and are paying for that experience. Especially if you come from a more limited upbringing or social background, the idea of going to a university and getting to know different people with a plethora of backstories can be exciting.

Just like the professional network, we have to ask ourselves if this is the best way of acquiring this experience.

Want to know how you can get the college experience without all the debt and opportunity cost? Just move to a college town and participate in intramural clubs and competitions. Plenty of people do this. They either move there hoping to become students someday but never enroll, or simply go for a few years to experience the life and culture with no intention of enrolling. It's an easy way to get a big part of why most people attend school in the first place.

But maybe you aren't just looking for the parties and the sporting events. Maybe you're looking to expand your social networks and looking for new experiences.

If you're a bright, driven young person, it isn't easy to go out and meet new people, especially if you are forced to do so through some other obligation. School forces us to meet each other by placing us within certain social confines. Work can do the same. Joining a high-growth team that requires a dynamic young worker is one easy way of expanding your social networks. Another is actually forcing yourself to meet people.

In *The Four Hour Workweek*, Tim Ferriss challenges readers to ask for the phone numbers of several strangers of the opposite sex. Even if you aren't actually interested in dating them, he says, asking for their numbers will make it much easier to initiate conversations elsewhere in life. Putting yourself outside your comfort zone allows you to shed the self- and other-imposed blinders that keep you from realizing just how easy many supposed difficulties are to overcome.

So go out there and try meeting four new people, using nothing but looks alone. You'll be astonished at how easy it is. Even if you get rejected, you'll learn through failure how to adapt your ways.

"What if I just want to learn?"

Let me be clear: I am not opposed to education. It is my love of education that drove me away from school. In a culture as thoroughly schooled as modern America, where most everybody has gone through compulsory K-12 education and more are going through seemingly compulsory college education, it can be difficult to differentiate between "education" and "school." It can be even harder to differentiate between "school" and "classes."

Not all education is schooling, and not all classes are schooling. For some people, classes are the best way to learn, but this doesn't mean they have to be enrolled in school in the traditional sense. For many, education and schooling are at odds with each other, with schools designed to produce a different result than what the individual wants to get out of his education.

If you are looking at staying in school because you want an education, you again must ask yourself, "College compared to *what?*"

You need not be a radical autodidact to find that school does a terrible job educating. From social pressures to majoring in "marketable" subjects to putting assignment minutiae before learning as a whole, schools create and reinforce incentive systems that make it difficult to focus on education first and foremost.

The great thing about the rise of the Internet is that it has lowered the barrier to entry for so many fields. Your cell phone has more human knowledge available to it than all of the libraries of Harvard circa1960. You just have to find a way to sort out that knowledge. This is what MOOCs (Massively Open Online Courses) like Coursera try to do. By having experts sort through and organize the available knowledge in a variety of fields, MOOCs make education open to anybody with an Internet connection. With degree-mills like the University of Phoenix taking advantage of this technology, "online education" gets a bad rap. People imagine somebody who didn't have what it takes to get into a "real college" sitting at home and doing their courses in their underpants. Whether this reputation is deserved is beside the point. What matters is this: if *education* matters to you, can this serve as a viable alternative?

Possibly so.

But one of the claimed advantages of college is that it allows you to focus on studies and nothing else. You can be a student full-time and not have to worry about paying the bills or going to work, the story goes.

This might be the case, but that doesn't mean it is desirable.

Education and work shouldn't be easily divisible. Creating and enforcing an artificial barrier between the two just distances education from its application to our lives and makes us view work as a mere necessity. Both education and work are necessary, and both have major impacts on how we structure our lives.

Balancing work with education makes it harder to compartmentalize both, allowing for applications from one to travel to the other. Studying Bertrand Russell's philosophy of work can be great when you aren't working, but it can have life-altering impacts when you are working. Getting a good grasp of economics can appear valuable in the abstract, but it can mean the difference between staying in your current job and launching your startup when you are working.

It's time that we rethought the idea that education and work are to be divided. We get the most out of both when we experience them concurrently.

For some people academia is the best place both to learn and work, and they feel comfortable in school. If you are still reading this chapter, you probably aren't this kind of person (or you have a morbid curiosity of why people want to tell others it is okay to leave school). If you are this kind of person, great! You'll do great in school. Go become a professor. Just don't tell others they have to follow your path.

"My parents won't let me drop out."

Parents of young people are some of the most ardent believers in the American collegiate mythos. They saw progress happen as more people got college degrees. They saw their friends go off to college and come back to phenomenal jobs. They saw college *work*.

Or so they thought, at least.

Even if college was the ideal way for a young person to take control of his life in that generation, this doesn't mean that it would be for a later generation. Like every generation before them, the boomers are afraid to let their children participate in something they -- the parents -- view as risky.

Their objections are motivated by love and concern -- but they don't have to constrain you.

One of the best ways to prove to your parents that you will not fail to achieve anything or be motivated in the real world is to take a leave of absence from school. Take a semester or a year off; get a job at a fast-growing company; find a mentor; or travel the world successfully and show them that you can not only take care of yourself outside of school, but you can flourish while doing that. Once you do this, their resolve will likely weaken, and you will be able to convince them more easily that you should drop out.

If they're still adamant, and you are sure you want to drop out, go ahead and do it anyway. Don't do it to be hostile or confrontational with your parents. Do it to show them that you are behind your commitment 100 percent. Do it to show them that while you respect their opinions, you can think for yourself. Do it to enforce your ownership rights over your own decisions.

Even if they are upset and angry in the moment, they're likely to come around as you flourish without school.

"I want to drop out. I just don't know where to start."

Okay, you're ready to get started, but you don't know where to turn. You may not have a mentor you can call on immediately to ask for a job, or you don't have your own idea that you can launch.

That's okay.

Getting started is hard. Just as in physics, an object at rest requires action by an outside force before it starts moving. Once you start moving, you'll be astonished at how easy it is to keep moving.

If you're looking to drop out and take control of your education and your career, but don't have a project to jump into immediately, your first goal should be identifying something you think you would enjoy. But how do you know what to pick?

Think about the things you *hate*.

Now think of all the jobs you could work in where you would be doing those things you hate as seldom as possible.

Find a company near you that you think does something interesting and inspirational, a company for which you would be happy to wake up in the morning and go to work. Find the highest-ranking person in that company and write an email explaining your background, experience, and reasons for wanting to work there.

Make your request clear: let me work for you.

If you must work for free first, do it (see below). Even if it is just a few hours per week, working for free and doing good work will not only ingratiate you with the team, but it will also put them in a position where, as time goes on and your opportunity cost rises with your increasing skill and experience, the company will be forced either to offer to pay you or find a replacement for you. Turnover costs are high, especially at startups, and replacing good talent is incredibly difficult even at entry level. Making yourself indispensable is your first step towards landing a job.

But how to make yourself indispensable? If you've been in school your entire life, you probably lack even the most basic workplace skills. How are you supposed to compete with people who might have more experience, connections, or a degree?

The most valuable skill is basic competence.

From executive vice presidents to summer interns, organizations often have a difficult time finding people who will do what they say they will do, show up when they say they will show up, and do their work well.

If you can approach your work singlemindedly for a short period of time and make yourself indispensable, you'll never have a hard time getting a paid full-time job.

If you have a skill, especially one in high demand like coding, sales, or a trade, simply make that clear when you email someone about work.

"But what if I don't get a reply?"

Be persistent. Send an email every week insisting on an interview and emphasizing that you can prove your worth. Worst-case scenario? You don't get a reply and learned how to be persistent in emails. Best case? You land the job.

Send emails to several companies. Showcase your work. Make your request clear. Don't ramble about different things you could do. Ask if you can work with them.

This will be your first step towards escaping school and being in the driver's seat of your education and career.

A modest proposal

Every year thousands of families will open up their pocketbooks and tap into the sacrosanct savings fund that many parents set up before their first child was even born: the college fund. As they prepare to send their high school graduates off to college, they'll shell out thousands of dollars to universities, housing companies, and textbook publishers – maybe symbolically giving the money to the student first, but with the clear understanding that it can then only be given directly to the universities. This money will support the student through the college years and help him launch himself forward into stable adulthood, offsetting any student loans he may need and making life a little bit easier.

Perhaps more romantically, the money is to provide the young person *opportunity*. Any good parent wants to give his children the opportunity to become their best possible selves. The most obvious and safest path to this in the mind of the boomers is to attend college. Go and learn about the world for a few years; try something new; and at the very least, even if you don't find a job on graduating, *you'll have a good experience and a degree under your belt*.

But this is the romanticized vision of the college experience. As I've said, in a world of *so much more information*, so much more (*cheap!*) connectedness, and *generally more opportunities for ambitious young people*, there's a huge opportunity cost to just taking the college-as-success pill no-questions-asked.

But even more, there's the huge financial cost to the college savings fund. If the purpose of saving up so much money ($10,000, $20,000, $50,000, maybe upwards of $100,000) is to use it so that your child may learn how to become a successful adult and be exposed to the experiences that will mold him as such, giving that money directly to a college is one of *the worst* possible things you could do.

Imagine that rather than giving this money to a university to cover tuition, parents instead took the money and gave it to their child as a "coming-of-age fund." The stipulations are simple: the newly christened adult can spend it on whatever he would like. If he wants to spend it on college, he is free to do so. But he is also free to spend it on a fancy car, a down payment on a house, traveling around the world, or seed-funding his own company. It would give him the freedom to explore his options without feeling pigeonholed.

Would some people take the money and blow it? Absolutely. Would others make something greater out of it than if they had spent it on college? Absolutely. What matters is that these young adults would actually be treated as adults and given the freedom and responsibility to deal with freedom and responsibility.

Even in the worst-case scenario, where a young person blows the money on sheer thrills and gambling, he would still learn more about himself and about managing money than if he were subsidized to sit in an academic bubble for four years, where he rarely felt the pain of spending $10,000 per semester so the university vice provost to the assistant secondary dean of diversity student life could afford a new Mercedes-Benz.

The college savings fund appears to be a great idea in the abstract – a sort of safety net to help push children of boomers onto the path to the middle class – but when considered with the opportunities it closes off and the other ways the money could be spent, it is a vestige of a risk-averse generation. Giving young people the opportunity to spend large sums of money however they wish would teach them more about themselves, the world around them, and the opportunities they do and do not have better than going to college simply because that's what they've been told to do.

You do you

Ultimately, the decision to drop out of school is a highly personal one, which can be fraught with waves of emotions thanks to a culture that glorifies the collegiate experience. I did not write this chapter to convince you to drop out of school if you love school. I wrote it for the people who, like me, feel that they can get something more out of the best years of their lives. I also wrote it because the cultural narrative around school is mind-bogglingly unfair. If you announce you are going to college, not a person will tell you to check yourself and make sure you aren't making a rash decision. If you announce you're going to drop out of school, you'll get stern talking-to from your parents and an email from your aunt you haven't seen in years; your friends may refer you to the school therapist. I want to flip that narrative.

Be very discerning about what you do while you are young. Being 18-25, with little debt, no mortgage, and no strong familial commitments gives you a level of freedom that very few other people have. You can try many things, take many risks, put a lot on the line without losing too much.

Leaving school isn't easy, and it is different depending on where you live. Being a dropout in Silicon Valley isn't as interesting as being one in Pittsburgh, Pennsylvania. People may discount you. People may not care. Prove them wrong. Make them esteem you by doing good work.

Don't put your life on autopilot at this stage. Take control of your career and your education, whatever that means for you. For me that meant going out and creating the educational experience I wanted in the real world. If that resonates with you, then I hope this chapter has served its goal.

Chapter Two

Why haven't you moved to a new city?

Ben and Nicole Angelo

For all its material advantages, the sedentary life has left us edgy, unfulfilled. Even after 400 generations in villages and cities, we haven't forgotten. The open road still softly calls, like a nearly forgotten song of childhood. –Carl Sagan

A little about us

In July 2013 we abruptly informed our customers we were closing *i heart ipanema*, our fashion and record store in Kalamazoo, Michigan, and moving to Los Angeles. We had no plan, no savings, no jobs, and no place to live in LA. Hey, weren't our optimistic declaration and gut feeling enough?

We'd been examining a move from every angle for a few months. The question had kicked around between us for years but never seemed to hit us simultaneously: should we move to a new city? We weren't sure how we could make it happen, but we knew ourselves well enough; we'd need a specific kind of motivation. If we need to clean the house, we plan a cocktail party. If we want to open a store, we start renting a retail space. So we plastered the announcement on our website and lit the fuse on our dream.

We were both ready for a change of scenery and a change of weather when Nicole went on her dear friend Alyson's bachelorette weekend to Big Sur and LA. Imagine a minivan full of beautiful, bright, and talented ladies (four of whom were transplants, and of those four, three from the Midwest) on a six-hour drive up the Pacific Coast Highway, all inquiring why you hadn't made the leap and informing you of every benefit of California living.

After Alyson showed me (Nicole) the best in vegetarian restaurants, specialty coffee, Venice, the culture, the people, I realized I wanted to have this every day. So I'm making phone calls back home to Ben saying things like "I don't know why we don't already live here" and "Everywhere I go it reminds me of you." Ben is really cool, and the things he is into are all here. I told him we'd talk about it more when I came home. I ended the call with "Don't tell anyone, but we need to talk about the possibility of moving here."

Towards the end of the life-changing trip, Alyson goes on video with arms open wide as the sun sets upon the hillside of Echo Park and exclaims, "Ben, you are moving to LA!" Ben was delighted by the prospect, so we decided we wanted to, and we decided we could.

The process

When our hearts were committed to moving to Los Angeles, we found Ben a job in his field. Once we had the job secured, we had about a week to move out of our apartment, re-sign the tenants on the rental property we owned, and close a fully functioning retail store. Let's not get into the brief but intense week-long legal entanglement with our draconian landlord who changed our locks when he found out we wanted to close the shop. That ate up one of our precious prep weeks. Once we regained access, we sold our furniture on social media to finance the trip in one week's time. We could rebuy most of our furniture when we got to LA, and we only kept the one-of-a-kind items. Family and friends' assistance in packing and moving us in such a short time cannot be overstated. It would not have happened without them.

Lead-up

We were lucky enough to have a copy of the *Not For Tourists Guide to Los Angeles* (a hand-me-down from friends when they were downsizing to move to Portland). Pick up some info on your new city and start to paint yourself into the life there. Research what different neighborhoods have to offer. You're not the first one to do this, and the web is filled with testimonials and tips. We dug through these and kept the tidbits that made sense to us. We avoided a lot of pitfalls reading others' mistakes and advice.

The road trip to LA

We loaded up our Lexus, which had 250k miles on it (we loaded it twice after Ben discovered he could fit his turntables in), borrowed an air mattress from the folks, and headed west. We made sure to get a tune-up and our tires and brakes checked out.

When your car serves as your camper and your seats, in their full upright and locked position with no wiggle room, become your bed at truck stops, you may become extremely ornery with yourself and your fellow traveler. This too shall pass, and when you look back at this rogue road trip it will be all sunshiny and glossy, and you will remember with fondness your renditions of Waylon Jennings's "Don't Let the Sun Set on You in Tulsa" while entering that fair city, the "they don't seem real" views of the Grand Canyon, and things of that nature.

But also you may remember your spouse using the sprinkler at the Route 66 Historic Rest Stop as a showerhead to wash his hair and the groundskeeper walking over swiftly to yell at him to put the sprinkler down.

Nicole realized this may have been her first time using the great outdoors (hey, she has camped, but only where there are restrooms available) when number-one hit just as the government shut down all the parks and, in the middle of nowhere, the bathrooms were closed. This is all part of the road-trip magic that gets you from point A to point B.

If you have the time, give yourself the gift of a road trip, complete with singing in the car, windows down, hair blowing in the wind, stops wherever the heck you please, and no real plan except getting to the new city.

When you arrive at your new city

You may end up using an air mattress as your chair, couch, and bed for months on end in your new space. That's okay. Not having a refrigerator or stove for a significant amount of time is survivable. Put up some things you love and browse Craigslist for give-aways. People-magnet cities have populations that are in constant flux. Someone is always moving, and you can benefit. Skip Ikea and hop online to find a treasure trove of things those folks don't want to move or don't need. Get some stuff to humanize your life (plants, chairs, art, a table), and tell yourself you can always replace it with the new new new when you get a stake.

This doesn't sound too glamorous, but this is real life! How badly do you want it? We made the move and remind ourselves all the time that we are making it in LA! You get on your feet, start to establish yourself, and settle in to the new life. We are now going through boxes because after a year and a half we had the time and money to go back to Michigan to get our belongings out of storage. We said we would, and we did -- a feeling of accomplishment. Our home is starting to feel like our home.

To move or not to move

Do not wait for permission. The first thing most people must do is flip the "I can't" switch to "I can" in your head. You (collective you if you're with a partner) are allowed to steer your own life in whatever direction you want. You need to. It's not up to your parents, your community group, your friends, your team, boss, department, alma mater, sorority, neighbors, country, anyone, really. You should definitely stop suffering unnecessarily and treat yourself to the things this world has to offer. If it's some kind of provincial loyalty anchoring you ("I'm just a Michigan guy"), remind yourself how your family wound up wherever you're from. At some point in history an ancestor of yours decided to move there for an opportunity at happiness from another place that their ancestors had moved to for the same pursuit. Plus, it's pretty much our heritage in the States. Go west! Get moving.

Where to go

Both of us are the kind of people who take a trip somewhere in the world and fall in love with the culture, the people, the food. But LA was like that to a greater extent because it already represented who we were and the things that resonate with us. We are deep into music + fashion + coffee + sunshine + health, and LA offered that. The lure of sunshine for days made our brains feel happy just thinking about it. Find a place that supports who you are. Are you a vegan? Then find a place that has a good farmer's market and at least one vegan restaurant. Do you love all four seasons? Find a place like Kalamazoo or Chicago, where you can participate in that. Do you love big-city living with skyscrapers and the subway? Well, then, LA wouldn't be for you.

What's the worst that could happen?

Whether it is weather, people, food, or the overall culture of a place you are dreaming of moving to -- just try it. What's the worst-case scenario? You decide you don't like the new city, your job there doesn't work out; you're homesick, and you decide to move back to where you came from. Well then at least you gave it a chance and can speak to the what-if yourself. Even if that happened, you would have lived through it and become more apt, with all your newfound knowledge, to try moving to a new city again sometime. Best-case scenario: it changes your life completely for the good, and you feel like you are becoming more yourself. Your outlook on life is more promising. Your mind is expanding. And you gain further understanding of yourself and others. Maybe the best is yet to come, and it could only come by being in this new city. That's what has happened to us!

The why behind moving

It's possible the city you grew up in no longer supports your ideals. You may have had job changes. Friends moved away. You went through a big break up. There are countless reasons at times. But the only reason you need is a need for change.

Think of how the new city would support you, your dreams, your ideals, etc.

The first year (honeymoon, homesickness & happiness)

We heard somewhere that if you made it through one year in a new city, you've beaten the homesickness and challenges and will able to stay there. Although this was our first time moving away, we were mentally prepared by that concept. Not only *could* we face powerful homesickness, we most likely would. Brace yourself. We're not trying to advise distracting yourself from the problem by joining social groups and such, although that could alleviate the feelings. You have made a radical change! Embrace it. Things are different, and that can be unsettling and mixed up for a while. If you're bummed and used to have lunch with your friends every Tuesday, check if it's a Tuesday.

We like to remind each other of a few things we love about our new spot and how we felt before the move. We tell each other it's a passing and common emotion to miss people. Hug a pillow and cry it away.

Oddly, this type of thing is where other languages are more honest about what is happening. In English we actuate and reinforce an incorrect identity of ourselves by saying things like "I am depressed." It sounds like you and "depressed" are interchangeable and that is interred in your psyche each time you think and say it. You are accidentally brainwashing yourself while trying to express and identify your emotional state at the moment. In Spanish, for instance, things subject to change (like emotions and the weather) are described using the verb *estar* (I am) ... *estoy triste* ... I'm sad right now. This is describing a transitory condition. It will change. It's not the same for the permanent assessment of conditions using the verb *ser* (I am)... *soy triste* ... I am inherently and unchangingly sad (or even "I am sadness!"). We should learn to think the Romance-language way. It correctly points out we will not be sad at some point in the future.

Be sure you are identifying a condition and not self-identifying as the condition. You're experiencing homesickness, and later you'll be experiencing joy. And just so there's no confusion, the emotions are not mutually exclusive. Also, we're living in the years that *Back to the Future II* was set in. Video-call your moms from your pocket TV-camera-phone! We spent our first Christmas on the beach Facetime-ing with our freezing loved ones. It was pretty magical.

FAQ ("What about X?" clearinghouse)

Can I make this a reality?
Yes!

Write it down in present tense: I am moving to _____.
Please apply liberally to any goal. It somehow makes sense to your brain. Whatever you dream or want, write it down in the present. Nicole has accomplished many of her goals with this little mind trick.

Do I need money saved up?
No!

You don't need hefty savings to move to a new city. We had literally no savings. Nicole used social media to list and sell our furniture in about one week's time. You do what you have to do! That was done to have money for the road trip and for living expenses. If you have savings – great! But it's not necessary to move. Selling your furniture is important for several reasons. One, you get quick cash. Two, you don't spend money storing your furniture until later. Three, you don't spend money later to move it across country. You can buy new/used furniture when you are able to. We were in a time crunch to move due to Ben's job. If family gives/loans you some cash for your road trip, humbly accept it.

Do I need a place to live before moving?
No!

We literally figured it out on the one-week road trip out there. Our backup plan was staying at a long-term hotel or campground. Listen, if you want it bad enough, your move will not be based on cushy circumstances. We were lucky enough to stay with Ben's siblings who had moved out to LA two weeks before, and we stayed there two weeks while we found a place. That was super gracious of them! This was a miraculous turn of events, since we all weren't planning the move together; that's just how it worked out. You may have friends or family you can crash with. If you don't know anyone where you are moving, that's no problem. Look into extended-stay hotels, Airbnb, or even local campgrounds. If determined, you can find a permanent place to rent in two weeks. Craigslist is what Nicole searched on day and night until she found a sweet flat to live in. A good reason to wait to find a permanent place until you are in your new city is that you will want to look the place over and check out the neighborhood. If you have the luxury of visiting the new city ahead of time and locking a place in ... kudos to you!

Should I look into places to live and neighborhoods before moving?
Yes!

Scope out prospective living quarters with a larger picture in mind. Where's the nearest grocery store, gas station, bank, record shop, boutique, movie theater, coffee shop, park, corner store? Study maps and read about the communities before moving. This will give you some insight into where to look. There are places you've got to go to all the time -- you want as many close by as possible. Commuting time is a big one when considering living options. In a place like LA your nine mile commute could take you one hour Be mindful of the traffic sitch.

Do I need a job lined up?
Yes!

Unless you have decent savings to live off of while you look or a partner who has secured a job, you'll need to make some cash to support yourself. In our case Ben had a job lined up -- Nicole found him a job in his field -- and Nicole didn't. (Nicole is a super-sleuth and somehow found me the best job before it was posted. --Ben) We drove out in less than a week's time and arrived as the sun was setting in LA. Ben went to work the next day and didn't look back. His determination and hard work are what got us through the first year and half.

Do I need others approval to make a big move?
No!

The only approval you need is your own, as you are the one who can determine your happiness. You are a grown up! For goodness's sake, stop people-pleasing to win the love of others! This is a message to you and to us. Really determine what you want from life, and go for it!

Will I be homesick?
Yes!

Be prepared to miss others and the familiarity of home. Nicole was definitely shedding some tears within the first year and having near panic attacks. Ben's first night in LA consisted of reuniting with his two brothers and freaking out at what they'd all just done. You will miss people and places, but that doesn't mean you made the wrong decision! It does mean you are getting into your rhythm of your new surroundings, learning about the city you chose, the people, and yourself. Finding your new favorite restaurants, grocery stores, the post office, coffee shops, and best modes of transportation takes time. Think back on the things that made you happy and unhappy in the city you came from. Then weigh in with the reasons the new city is making you happy.

Will I make it?
Yes!

You will make it in the new city if you aren't counting on having all of your luxuries. You may have to use the borrowed air mattress as your only furniture for some unsaid months like we did. But in the end it's worth it! The bottom line is this: how bad do you want the change in your life. Are you willing to sacrifice for possibly over a year while you establish yourself in this new city? The new developments and experiences in your life will reaffirm in your heart that you are making it. What has this move done for you? Who have you met? What new experiences bring life to you? Our move to LA has brought experiences and people into our lives beyond our wildest imagination. A favorite experience was befriending Money Mark of Beastie Boys, a keyboard legend, whose Latin-tinged soul-jazz tracks (collected on *The In Sound From Way Out!*) helped shape Ben's musical explorations. We met him in a cafe in LA.

How long should I stay in the new city if I'm feeling uncertain?
At minimum, one year—no matter how hard it gets. Prove to yourself you can do it, and give it a shot—one year! After one year, you will know if it is where you belong and whether you're thinking emotionally or practically.

Should I tell others about my plans to move as soon as I think of it?
No!

Resist the desire to tell others you're thinking about it until you are ready to commit to your own idea and ready to defend it. Ask friends or relatives who have moved to share their experiences. They'll be friendly to the topic and won't kill it with horror stories: EARTHQUAKES ... TRAFFIC ... SMOG ... HOLLYWOOD ... $$$. Once you say it, know that there could be some negative responses. But so what? Who cares what others say? You are already committed to your idea at that point.

Someone close to us had the kind of response we just described. How could we think of it? We were already in the planning phase and had no trouble looking this person in the eye and standing up for ourselves by saying that we needed this for our own happiness. That stopped the comments. Later, he confided that after thinking it over, he just was so sad we were going away and hoped we'd change our mind. He ultimately loved us enough to back us up.

A more preemptive approach could help, like telling those you care about how you will keep in touch and planning with them to do so. If you tell your best friend you'll be on the video chats with her every Sunday, she'll feel way less like you're abandoning her.

Should I put my belongings in storage?
Yes!

If there are sentimental things such as photos, vinyl records (boxes upon boxes), art pieces, and other things that will not fit into your car, put them in storage, ideally with family or in rental unit. We did both. You can safely assume we had a lot of things after having a home, an apartment, and a store and music studio. When will you get them? You will when you are able to. We reunited with our belongings after a year and a half in storage, loaded up some shipping containers from U-Haul, and had everything shipped to LA, then flew back. It met us there in a week in the same condition it left. Pretty simple.

Conclusion

This is the story of how we changed our lives. It's never too late to steer the ship in a different direction. Your ideas, ideals, hopes, and dreams are of utmost importance. The bottom line is your own. You will make or break yourself. Care enough about your own happiness to move to a new city if that's what it takes. The concept of happiness is a complex one and is easily oversimplified. I wonder how many of us have truly and honestly opened ourselves up to learning what sustained and lifelong happiness means to us and what it takes to have that kind of existence. It's a topic for lifelong exploration, but we've found that in opening ourselves up this way, we feel the most *ourselves* that we have ever felt. For some, moving to a new place helps people reinvent themselves. For others it confirms everything about who they are. When you live in a place that supports your entire being and understands you, it's hard to describe the feeling.

Chapter Three

Why haven't you written a book?

Jeffrey Tucker

Maybe it is time for you to write a book. Publishing has never been easier. You might sell some copies. You might make a difference in someone's life. Regardless, being an author amounts to redefinition of who you are and what you have to offer the world. In some ways it is an act of bravery. There's no better time than now, provided you are ready and have something to say.

Here's a history of my own book writing.

I used to think that books were for big shots. They were surely exhausting to write. They had to say an epic and stunning thing. They had to shoot for best-seller status. They should include a tremendous number of citations, for "credibility." They had to be vetted. I also avoided putting one together out of fear. Once something is in a book, you have to be responsible for the contents. Books define you. I didn't want to be defined. So I waited, much too long.

Finally in 2009, I did it. I discovered a theme in my writings. That theme was creative noncompliance with prevailing social, cultural, and political *diktat*. In article after article, I had (inadvertently) chronicled the many small ways in which we can be rebels in our own lives. I found that I was comfortable with that theme because it was highly personal -- something over which I had unique knowledge. No, there was no big idea, no plan for the world economy, no gigantic philosophical message, no earth-shattering insight. But there was an interesting bit of inspiration here, and the essays were all rather engaging.

I collected them, edited them, tied them together, and there it was. The result was suitable. Maybe someone would care. In any case, by putting it out there I could close one chapter in my life. That sounded appealing.

The next step was to find the title. That was the hard part. It tooks months of reflection. I tried dozens but nothing was quite right. Then I recall the first moment in my adult life when I gained some sense that I could live dangerously in small ways. It was an early morning, talking to an older gentleman in the deep South. He poured me a cup of coffee and asked if I wanted bourbon in it. I was stunned because I had somehow come to believe, and I don't know why, that morning drinking was something that one should never do, no matter what.

This was a revelation to me, and since this book was deeply personal, I decided to highlight the event in the title. Hence: *Bourbon for Breakfast*. The book appeared, and I had no inkling of what would happen next. It sold well, very well. And then, out of nowhere, I became known for it. The title defined my life. The essays in there -- many simple life hacks and various reflections on the problems of government regulation -- went viral. It inaugurated something else that I did not expect. I became a public personality. I had never been that before, and this did indeed redefine others' perceptions of me and those of myself and my role.

It was all due to the book. Many others have followed, including *It's a Jetsons World*, *Beautiful Anarchy*, *Liberty.me*, and *Bit by Bit*, among three others, along with about 150 book introductions and many chapters in books. In the years that followed, my career took a completely different turn. I went from being a code geek and editor in a small office, a life in which no one knew my name, to being a public figure. It dated from that one book.

Why did my first book succeed? It had a good title. It had a good distribution network. The content was readable. Above all else, I think the reason that the book did well was that it was personal. That's another way of saying that it was original -- and because no one else has lived your life, the personal is necessarily original. I had managed to embrace the one thing that I did really well, which is live a slightly eccentric life in light of an oddball political philosophy, and I put it out there for people to read. I had not attempted to do more than that.

What should your book be about?

Leaving the think-tank world, I entered into the for-profit publishing business in which I sorted through many manuscripts to consider them for publication. I was always happy to get these, and I would congratulate anyone who finished a book for publication. But I rejected most of them. A surprising number of these books were of the same sort: they were sweeping introductions to some gigantic topic like human liberty. They attempted to start at the beginning and go to the end. They were didactic, always trying to school the reader in what he or she should think.

I was polite as possible with such people but, in one way or another, I ended up telling the writer the same thing: no one wants to read this. This book is a duplicate of information anyone can find on the Internet in a matter of minutes. It is a summary of what you learned from Googling. It adds no value to the world. There is nothing wrong with self-publishing, and it's fine and not awful to go ahead. But there is something inauthentic -- purely derivative and notably bloodless -- about the structure and message of such a book. It will not accomplish what you want it to accomplish. The truth is that no one needs yet another general introduction to libertarianism. So sorry.

If not that, what should your book be about? In some sense, it doesn't matter. What does matter is that it is real, not affected, not a put-on, not a phony attempt to sound like someone other than who you are. Books I would like to read are about real things: the underground history of real life in high school; the truth about the Greek system in college; what it is like to have your first job; experiences in dealing with extended family and their expectations. Fears. Hopes. Adventures. Whatever. The story line doesn't matter so much as its authenticity.

Notice that all my suggestions here are autobiographical. All truly excellent first books are autobiographical. It's the way writers get their feet wet. Only later do they venture into more abstract areas. First you need to train yourself to write what you are absolutely certain is the truth, as much as you can know the truth. Once you do that, you can extend that model outward. Taking that first step is the key. You need to come to believe that what you think about something that you know really does matter.

In fact, take a look at this chapter. I was assigned an essay about book writing. I could have begun with a big theory, a list of dos and don'ts, a mighty essay on the history of books, or whatever. If I had done that, you probably would have stopped reading by now. By choosing the tactic of laying out my personal story, confessing some vulnerabilities that you share, you felt engaged and you kept reading. There is a lesson here.

There is always something vulnerable about this kind of writing. You feel it as you do it. Maybe you feel a bit squeamish. Even shy. This is good. The reader will feel that too and become sympathetic to your voice. To be a reader is to be a bit of a voyeur of another person's inner life. As a writer, you need to be prepared to share that life. It doesn't have to be about you overtly, but it should draw from that which you know best, and that means yourself.

Fear of the reader

In my experience the hardest thing for any writer to overcome is fear of the reader's reaction. You don't know who is going to be reading. Is it mom? Your professor from college? Your boss? Your social circle? Your pastor? You are a different person to each of these groups. When you write a book, you are only one person to all these people. Which person do you want to be? Whom do you want to impress? Just thinking about this creates terrible anxieties. People sit in front of blank computer screens all day just turning such issues over in their minds.

How do you overcome that fear of the audience? It really is a fear of yourself, of not being able to find and settle on your voice. Deciding on that takes some serious personal reflection. You need to commit -- not for all time, but just for this one time as you write. You can change later. We all mature and grow. But for this one book, you need to find yourself. Sometimes imagining a single reader can help you do that. A friend, a family member, a beloved mentor, a protege, a younger person setting out on a similar life path. Maybe that audience you imagine doesn't really exist, and you create it just for the purpose of this book. That works too. But you will need to settle on it and stick with it for the duration.

What about writer's block? What happens when you just can't think of anything to add, or anything to say? I once asked the great economist Henry Hazlitt about this. His response was that he could never afford to have writer's block any more than a bicyclist can have pedaler's block. It was just something he did and had to do every day. He would not allow himself not to write. That's an interesting way to think about it.

And yet, let us be realistic. We do run out of ideas. The words do stop flowing suddenly, and we get stuck. How to fix that problem? I often use external objects and experiences to kick up my creativity. I look outside and focus on one thing that is happening. I examine it, think about the implications and their meaning, find something in that object or event that is a bit unusual or interesting, and then I try to relate it to other things. This process can be delightfully disruptive in the best way; it can "get the cobwebs out."

You return to your computer a bit fresher and ready for work. I did that just now, and, sure enough, thought of something else I want to add on this point. I went outside and saw a hose watering some flowers. The stream of water reminded me of the flow of creativity. Ideas are the water molecules. There is an infinite supply of them, forever. Never doubt that. Ideas are not scarce. Never fear that they will run out. There is nothing you can do to cause them to dissipate, and there is no reason to fear a future in which they do not exist.

Your main task is to find the ideas that entice you, describe them, apply them in interesting ways, use them to illuminate the world and life in a way that brings new focus and clarity.

As you write, remember that everything you say can be changed. There is no reason to feel attached to prose just because you wrote it. My father used to tell me to write my essays and then delete the first paragraph. That's because all young writers have a tendency to build in long runways before getting to the thing we want to say. I did that for years, until it became habitual to begin with the action item, as a way of immediately starting with the thing that people care about.

Use your best ideas now

Young writers also have a tendency to hold back on their best material until they believe the reader is prepared for it. It also stems from a fear that once the best material is used up, there will be nothing else to write. This really is a mistake. Often it is best to start with your best material, your best statement of the theme, your best-possible idea, and then explore where that leads you. You might find that you will discover more as you write and think.

If you have ever listened to a Brahms violin or cello sonata, this is exactly what he does. The sonata begins with the theme, immediately, stated completely and fully in its most developed form. Very quickly, even before the themes is fully presented, it begins to move onward in new directions and new unexpected ways. You get the sense that Brahms had one idea, couldn't wait to put it down, and then this idea gave way to a slightly different one, and so on, and then he returns to find its essence and restate it in different ways, and so on. The listener is on a journey with the composer and player. What you find here is an amazing confidence in the truth of the music that he heard in his heart. And truly, he did just open his heart and pour it out onto the manuscript paper. As a matter of fact, most of this music -- most all great music -- was inspired by love (eros in this case).

And so, above all else, the writer of a book must learn to reveal his or her love, and not be shy about that. Writing that is not imbued with love does not engage. It's fine for an academic journal or technical manual. But it does not work for real readers. To love in prose, in public, for others in the hope of inspiring others to draw some inspiration from what you love, is the highest aspiration of any writer. Learning to do that is the great challenge we all face.

And yes, there is a vulnerability to doing this. But we grow when we take it on.

This is the number-one reason to undertake the project of book writer. It helps us become better people. It helps us find ourselves. More precisely, it helps us discover something new about ourselves, at least as we exist in this moment in time. And that's all a book can really do, capture a moment in the life of our own minds. There will be other moments, God willing, new thoughts, and new ideas. We can be confident in that. And when that moment comes, we can start book two.

Chapter Four

Why haven't you quit your job?

Peter Neiger

Chapter Four

"Looks like you've been missing a lot of work lately."
"I wouldn't say I've been 'missing' it, Bob" - Office Space

My sweat and tears merged as they poured down my face and the salty, dusty fluid dripped off my sun-cracked lips to the scorching pavement. I sat on the side of the road with my head in my hands as the New Mexico sun beat down on the back of my neck. I felt defeated by nature with all the energy sapped out of me. Even the wind, which was almost hot as it blew across the desolate highway, offered no relief. There was no shade in sight, and my muscles ached from weeks of cycling across over 2,000 miles. My body wanted to quit; my mind was nearing delirium; my very spirit felt drained; but the truth is I was so much happier than I had been in years. I knew the pain would eventually fade, but the feeling of control and freedom I had in my life would last forever. And really, it all started when I quit my job.

When I made the decision to quit my job and cycle from Washington, DC, to Los Angeles, I received a lot of negativity from my network in DC. On the surface, the decision seemed to be really foolish. I was only three years out of college, and I had a good job along a career path in economics. I had no other job offers or prospects within my field, much less on the other side of the country. I had over $65,000 in student loans and less than $1,500 in my checking account. Why I was comfortable giving up my job security to have an adventure and escape my unhappy but stable life was hard to explain. After all, aren't we supposed to wait until retirement (or maybe two weeks a year) to have adventures? Aren't our 20s and 30s for laboring as long as possible so that we can have enough money in the bank to buy an RV when we retire? I didn't really realize it at the time, but it started at Burning Man when I "flipped the burden of proof" about not only my job but also how society views work as a whole.

One of the principles of Burning Man is "Participation." You are encouraged to try new things and be an active participant in the community that comes together every year. In short you are asked to approach the world with "Why not?" on your mind instead of "Why?" Whether that means climbing up on an art car and dancing until sunrise, participating in a yoga class, or following a strange man in a chicken costume just to see where he leads you, you are encouraged to flip the burden of proof and come up with good reasons not to do something. There are always little excuses to opt out of a new experience, but our lives are not made richer by opting out, and the reasons for not trying new things should be strong. As with all of Burning Man's Principles, all burners are encouraged to continue pursuing them outside of Black Rock City as we move back into "the default world." While speaking with a friend at Burning Man about my dissatisfaction at work, it dawned on me that I should quit and do something adventurous. Why not?

Not everyone should quit his or her job. As was stated in the introduction to this book, there are legitimate reasons to stay within the status quo. The important step is to flip the burden of proof, to question everything in our lives on a regular basis to see what serves a purpose, and change those things that don't. To paraphrase what a former pastor of mine once said in a sermon, "Comfort is not good. Comfort is not the goal. Comfort is stagnation. We grow and gain strength through discomfort alone. Giving in to comfort is to accept stagnation, decay, and eventually death."

Few things in life are as comfortable as a job. It is often the foundation of our time and lives. We sacrifice everything and adjust our schedules around work before all else. For many people leisure, family, friends, and passion all come second to the cornerstone of employment. Disrupting your work can disrupt your whole life, but that disruption does not mean it is permanently destructive. In fact, this pedestal that we have placed jobs on means we should analyze it ever more closely to ensure it is providing the value it should. Foundations in your life should be held to a higher standard. They are too important to follow solely as a matter of tradition or social norms without individual scrutiny. A job itself is not somehow intrinsically good. It is only a good thing if it is creating value in our lives.

Before quitting my job I ran through the reasons I had a job to make sure it was filling its intended purpose. The answer to this will certainly differ depending on the person, but for me my job was not something I loved or was particularly passionate about. It paid the bills and provided me with a future. Both of these purposes needed to be evaluated.

Security

This was the obvious one. We have jobs to earn money so that we can be safe and secure. In our society we need an income to meet our basic needs. As Abraham Maslow pointed out,[9] if we don't meet the basic physiological needs for air, water, food, and shelter, we will be too focused on survival to pursue things like happiness, satisfaction, or love. If my job is the only way for me to get basic security in my life, then there is no way I could quit unless I had a new job lined up.

After some analysis I realized two things. First, meeting your basic food needs in the United States in the early 21st century is basically easier and cheaper than ever in human history. In 1900 Americans spent 30 percent of their income on food. Today that number is close to 10 percent.[10] And that isn't only because we are much wealthier than a hundred years ago (though we are); it is because food prices are down dramatically. Adjusted for inflation, a dozen eggs in 1930 cost $5.57; in 2010 the cost was $2.51.[11] I realized I didn't need a large income to thrive. I could cook for myself and eat healthily for about $400 a month.

Second, paying for shelter in Washington, DC, was a more serious problem. There was simply no way I could live in DC without my job. In fact I could barely afford to pay rent *with* my current job. The rent was so expensive that I couldn't save money in any meaningful way. If I wanted to quit my job I needed to take a leap without much of a safety net. Luckily for me, one of the main reasons I wanted to quit my job was the city it was in. The culture of my nation's capital was part of the poison in my life. It was what I needed to escape. Providing myself with shelter once I started biking turned out to be really cheap. You can camp many places for free simply by staying out of sight, or you can pitch a tent in state, county, or local parks for around $15 per night. There are also virtual communities (namely, CouchSurfing and Warm Showers) that provide travelers free places to sleep. Either way, that is way cheaper than paying for an apartment.

Basically, after some budgeting I realized I could shift my student loans to income-based repayment, quit my job (thus, having no income), and live off of my last paycheck for a couple of months while I bike across the country and see what life throws my way.

Future career

After thinking about survival, it was obvious that I had to consider how quitting would affect my future, particularly my career. Many philosophers, spiritual leaders, and significant scientific research have shown the benefits of living in the moment and not worrying about the future. Christ may have said it best in Matthew 6:34 (New International Version), "Therefore do not worry about tomorrow, for tomorrow will worry about itself. Each day has enough trouble of its own." In addition, the practice of meditation, which focuses on present mindfulness instead of thinking about the past or the future, has been shown to lower stress, increase self-awareness, reduce negative emotions, and assist with a variety of medical issues, including anxiety disorders, depression, heart disease, and general pain.[12] Similarly the Greek and Roman Stoic philosophers believed in focusing only the things that in their control instead of the past or the future:

> Work, therefore to be able to say to every harsh appearance, "You are but an appearance, and not absolutely the thing you appear to be." And then examine it by those rules which you have, and first, and chiefly, by this: whether it concerns the things which are in our own control, or those which are not; and, if it concerns anything not in our control, be prepared to say that it is nothing to you. --Epictetus

When I really started thinking about my future, I realized that much of it was out of my control, and the further in the future I planned, the less control I had. In this ever-changing world nearly any job is up for automation. The "career path" of the late 20th century may very well go the way of the Dodo, just like the industrial jobs of the middle of the century. In fact, work as an institution will likely keep shifting as more wealth is created and technology replaces people. Even white-collar careers like lawyers, accountants, and investors can be mostly replaced by algorithms. There is no reason to believe that couldn't apply to my job as well. None of us is guaranteed tomorrow, much less 40 years from now, and we are certainly not guaranteed good health 40 years from now. While I was biking across the country I heard a variation of the same thing from those older than me, "Good for you! I'm a bit jealous. It is good you are doing it while you are young, healthy, and don't have kids. I wish I would have done that in my youth."

This response from people, many of whom were retirement age or close to it, was similar to what palliative nurse Bronnie Ware found. In her 2012 book *The Top Five Regrets of Dying: A Life Transformed by the Dearly Departing*, she found that regrets seemed to focus on not living life to the fullest and not being true to yourself. In fact every male patient she researched said that he wished he hadn't worked so hard. People didn't regret going on adventures, trying new things, or taking risks. They regretted living their lives in a safe way that wasn't true to their own desires.

It seemed to be a better choice to diversify my experiences and maximize my leisure time. As a 2012 paper in *Journal of Experimental Psychology*[13] showed, new experiences and challenges increase an individual's creativity, as well as his ability to adapt to new situations (such as the creative destruction of a career). New experiences quite literally change who you are. Our consciousness and personality are largely impacted by our experiences.

This risk paid off for me. My two-month bike ride provided me with a fresh view of my own life, and I realized I was no longer interested in a career in economics. After arriving in Los Angeles I started working on the management side of an executive protection firm. My boss was not bothered in the least by my relatively short employment stints (two jobs over three years) or my gap in employment because of my bike ride. He didn't even mind me taking 10 days off of work during my first month so I could attend Burning Man. In fact he seemed to approve of my willingness to leave a job situation I wasn't happy with, and he recognized my diversity of experiences as an opportunity to create value. I had a unique perspective and unique experiences in life, which should be seen as a good thing.

I recognize that my situation was unique to me. Everyone is going to have a different risk-tolerance, different responsibilities in life, and a different level of discomfort in their current situation. For me quitting allowed me to take a life-changing adventure, but other opportunities await those who quit. Freeing up your time and exposing yourself to a new level of discomfort and risk create greater incentives to start a new business, focus on artistic creation, and see what you are made of. When you take that first step and quit your job, you no longer have the opportunity to put off your passion until tomorrow ... and you have the energy each day to create instead of being mentally exhausted.

Quitting turned out to be the right decision for me. As I write this I am in Green Bay, Wisconsin, in the middle of a 35,000 mile, three-year bike ride through the lower 48 states with my wife and dog. I am gainfully employed in a job where I work remotely and am more financially secure than I was in DC, thanks to the experiences and connections I made when I quit my job. Some people have jobs they love and are passionate about -- they wake up daily excited about their day -- but I was not one of those people. Instead of settling for the status quo I took a risk, quit my job, went on an adventure, and now I am living the life I want. None of the men and women I look up to spent their lives doing the 9-5. They created the life and wealth they wanted by pursuing their dreams.

When it comes down to it, the opportunity for a better life is in our own hands. I think Steve Jobs said it best:

> For the past 33 years, I have looked in the mirror every morning and asked myself: "If today were the last day of my life, would I want to

do what I am about to do today?" And whenever the answer has been "No" for too many days in a row, I know I need to change something.... [A]lmost everything – all external expectations, all pride, all fear of embarrassment or failure – these things just fall away in the face of death, leaving only what is truly important. Remembering that you are going to die is the best way I know to avoid the trap of thinking you have something to lose.

Chapter Five

Why haven't you started a business?

Levi Morehouse

My Story - Short Version

Since my mid-teens I knew I wanted to own a business. While the reasons were many, varied, and not totally clear, I wanted the challenge to see if I could do what others I respected had done in building something from zero to an IPO. I wanted the freedom to choose what to work on and how to be valuable. I wanted control. I wanted ultimately to be personally responsible for success, failure, or the murky in-between. I wanted to love what I did all the time, and I felt creating/building/owning it was the best way to do this. That was all I knew about it. I was unsure of what business. I did not have specific wealth or income goals. I simply knew that I wanted to create something. At that point it became my mission to start a business.

I have always been a practical person and also willing to work hard to get what I want. I went through college as quickly as possible, got an internship followed by full-time employment at a large CPA firm in my area, and started several side businesses. Doing all of these things allowed me to learn a lot, make a decent living, and explore my business aptitude. It also required that I worked nonstop, making me unable to fully focus on the entrepreneurial endeavors. As I moved through my early life I constantly kept my eye out for opportunities to get into business. I continued to take every opportunity I could to learn and define in more detail what "owning a business" was going to be for me.

After leaving the CPA firm to help grow a small business, I realized I was closer but still not quite there. Helping run a business was one thing, but I knew I wouldn't be satisfied until I did it myself. I set out on my own with a business idea that morphed into another, and finally into my current company, Ceterus. It was the scariest move I've made, and it required me to take a 70 percent pay cut, work all the time, and enter total uncertainty – all with a wife and three, then four, then five kids. To detail this journey a little further, I will provide the following timeline:

My Story - Long (Boring) Version

Throughout high-school and college I worked for an entrepreneur with a telecommunications business. The primary thing I did was to install network cabling in auto dealerships that were just adopting the Internet. I learned a great deal and had a lot of responsibility at a young age managing a small crew and getting the job done on time and on budget.

Perhaps what was more valuable in this experience was that the owner asked if I would moonlight and get the company's books in order. He handed me a copy of QuickBooks from 1998, and I worked through setting up the books, financials, and payroll processing on this system (usually while Napster was in the background downloading Pink Floyd and Moby over a 56k modem).

This gave me an incredible view into the workings of the business of business. Dealing with unemployment insurance, employer taxes, income taxes, workers compensation, customers who don't pay, vendors impatient for their money, and much more was invaluable in my discovering that the business of business is real, a little tricky, and necessary, but ultimately not an unsolvable mystery.

In the middle of my junior year I took a semester off and got a tax-season internship at a large CPA firm in the area. This was followed by a part-time job there the following tax season while completing my degree and a full-time position there post-graduation as a staff auditor. The firm experience was excellent. I earned my CPA license while there and also learned that, while it's an amazing profession, being a partner at a CPA firm was not going to allow me to scratch the entrepreneurial itch that had developed years earlier. At the firm I worked hard, worked many, many hours (common in that industry), did well, but also continued to search for business opportunities.

In reading about generating passive income and wealth and starting a business, I saw that many books recommended owning real estate. At 19 I jumped in, got a mortgage, and bought a tiny house for $54k. I lived in it for six months, then bought a second house for slightly more. I moved to the second house, rented the first, flipped the second, and moved to a third within the next year. I still own that first house today. I hate being a small-time landlord, and I learned not to start a business that you know nothing about just because others say it is a good move. (Note: *If anyone wants to buy a tiny house in Portage, Michigan, let me know* 😊) I learned that real estate as a business was not for me, but I don't regret that I took my first action towards building a business.

As I was looking for opportunities while working as a CPA, I got impatient and took the "known" route back to what I knew. I started a telecommunications business with a successful electrical contractor as a minority investor. I hired my recently graduated brother to run the business and traded in my newly purchased Honda Accord (first new vehicle ever) to buy a work truck.

Chapter Five

My brother used the truck for jobs, while I drove his air-condition-less $500 car to audits all over the state. I juggled this start-up while working 60-plus-hour weeks during tax season. On several occasions I ducked into a bathroom while on an audit to try to sell a new client on telecommunication installation over the phone. My brother eventually needed a more stable job, and I realized I could not really grow this business without being in it 100 percent. I ended up closing it down. I lost a small amount of money, spent a lot of time, and incurred a lot of stress from this venture. Ultimately those costs purchased me the lesson that it is really, really hard to be successful at something when you cannot give 100 percent to it.

With the telecommunications side-business not taking off and my real-estate empire dreams fading quickly, I realized that to really get where I wanted to go, I would need to leave the CPA world and venture into the world of running a business full-time. I opted for a really good opportunity in a refrigeration business. The idea was to work for 5-10 years with the owner and then buy into and potentially buy out the business. It was owned by my father-in-law, an excellent entrepreneur himself. What I learned in this position was valuable. In addition to maintaining the books, I helped develop a regulatory compliance service for customers, and I launched an international sales effort, expanding the parts business from the midwestern United States to every corner of the globe. Don't take this for more than it was: parts made up a small percentage of the company's revenues. Regardless, I gained incredible hands-on learning in many facets of business. After four years I was really itching to move forward with my ownership plans, and we decided my timeline was not going to work. This experience was great; however, it was now abundantly clear I would need to put 100 percent of my effort into something that was 100 percent my own from the start.

When I left the refrigeration business I decided it was time to start something. I opened a home-care business. I worked this business exclusively for six months with very moderate success. (The business still exists but is very small.) I had a family and took a 70 percent pay cut from my last year employed. While I saw that this business could potentially work, I also discovered that I was in this business to make a living on my own, not because I had any unique competitive advantage in it. I realized that I was 100 percent committed, 100 percent in charge, yet I was not uniquely talented at this work or passionate about the industry itself.

At the same time I realized I was not uniquely qualified to build a successful home-care business, it dawned on me that I actually loved the mundane details of setting up world-class accounting and financial-reporting systems in the cloud. I did this for my personal finances. I had done it for my start-ups. Heck, I had done it back in high school for my employer. Every small business I had been part of could have used a simple, affordable solution that not only told it how to run an accurate and efficient accounting system; it could use a company to do it for them. I thought this was fun, but I never considered it all that valuable to others. Then the revelation hit. I love this, I am good at this, and I think it could be something millions of entrepreneurs would benefit from. I immediately went about firming up my plan, attracting clients, and making this idea into a business. From the start I did not want a business built only on my unique interests and skills. I pushed constantly to make it a scalable business built on systems and processes to benefit millions of clients, not just the few I could personally work with. I knew I had found the right product/market/founder fit, and it felt amazing. The next five years were the hardest of my life: the hours were brutal, the stress off the charts, the financial risk high -- and I loved every minute. Since then I have assembled a world-class team, and empowered entrepreneurs across the country with niche-specific financial reporting and automated accounting by Ceterus.

It was crazy at first (and still is much of the time), but it was also the best thing I'd ever done. I don't think starting a business is for everyone, but I think a lot of people assume they can't do it without fully exploring the idea. I want to take an honest look at the pros, cons, costs, and benefits before asking: why haven't you started a business?

Do you have the itch?

Successful entrepreneurs are similar to movie stars, rock stars, and high-profile athletes right now. The American Dream of business ownership has always been a noble pursuit in this country, but the past decade has taken this to another extreme. Entrepreneurs simply owning their means to make a living has been replaced with large personalities starting businesses that change the world. Movies are being made about entrepreneurs and their companies just a few years into their existence.

I am a big fan of this trend. I enjoy articles, tweets, and news about entrepreneurs. I enjoy these more than political, celebrity, and even sports-related media. This glorification of the entrepreneur, or business owner/founder, is largely harmless or even a good thing.

While American culture has had a proclivity for entrepreneurship for a long time due to the independence it provides, as well as the potential financial rewards, entrepreneurship now also puts you into a high social status. I think this leads many people to feel that until they have tried to start their own business, they are missing out and are shorting themselves. I guess I am saying that many people in this country think they have "the itch" to be an entrepreneur. While some of this might be due to the previously mentioned glorification, the entrepreneurial itch certainly exists, and when you have it, it must be scratched.

Is the itch yours, or coming from forces around you?

If you feel the itch, it is smart to determine if it is truly your itch (internal) or if the culture is making you think you have the itch (external). There are ways to determine this. I suggest reading some of the many books on this topic. Be honest with yourself, and take action. Action can mean not scratching the itch and seeing if it goes away. Action can mean dropping everything and starting a business, and action can mean dabbling in a business while still doing other things. Regardless, you should determine if the itch is internal or external.

If it is real, why haven't you started a business?

If you have the itch and you are reasonably sure that it is internal, then the question becomes "why haven't you started a business?" I am always amazed at how many people talk about starting a business and take no concrete steps to do so. I am confident that many of these people feel the itch externally but not internally.

I am also convinced that some of them truly have the itch. They are the ones who perplex me. Why are they not moving forward? I have a strong natural bias to action, so but writing this has made me assess the question "Why haven't you started a business?" I have done my best to take this question seriously and see it from various perspectives. The remainder of this chapter will dig into what I feel are four potential reasons *not* to start a business.

After each section, I will conclude with a few scenarios and my specific advice for each.

Reasons not to start a business

"I Don't Know Anything about Business"
If you are considering starting a business, there is a good chance that you know a lot about whatever your business will do (the product or service you will provide), however, there are many things required on the *business* side of a business. I am referring to the set-up, legal issues, regulation, taxes, accounting, software, liability, lawsuits, and insurance. Most people are not experts in these things, and the *business* of starting a business can certainly be a reason *not* to start.

Why this might be true
While it varies industry by industry and location by location, it is true that in nearly every case, running a business will require handling some of the details listed above. This *business* of starting a business is a distraction from the true value provided by your firm, and it takes away from your ability to focus on the quality of your product or service, manage staff, drive growth, service customers, and improve profitability.

In addition to taking away from the value of your business, the *business* of a business is also what can get you in trouble. The threat of IRS liens and lawsuits cause stress and in some cases could land you in jail (though rarely). So while you may have the itch to do something, there is no escaping the fact that there is *business* with any business.

Why this might not matter
Among the many benefits of the time we are currently living in is very easy and affordable access to specialists through the Internet. It is possible to start a business and contract with specialists and providers who are experts in their respective components of the business side of things. Small-business entrepreneurs can enjoy the peace of mind formerly reserved for large and well-funded businesses. From outsourced accounting and bookkeeping (shameless plug for my business, Ceterus), to online legal forms, to lenders, insurance providers, and virtual assistants, all forms of scalable services are available online, payable monthly, to ensure your business side is covered with minimal upfront investment. While you will need to handle some of the complexity and achieve some understanding, many places can provide

affordable help and reduce the distraction, making the *business* of doing business simply a minor nuisance and not a reason to never get started.

Scenario 1: *"After learning of all the business that goes with starting a business, there is no way I could sleep well at night. Even with good help and outsourcing, the risks and hassles of these things scare me and would negatively affect my quality of life."*

This is an easy answer: Do *not* start a small business (perhaps a large well-funded business would be OK). It is very likely that you are not cut out for this. No matter what measures you take, the *business* of business will always pose threats, and it takes a certain person to manage a high-quality life in spite of this. If that is not you, there is no shame in it, so move to find what that itch really is telling you.

Scenario 2: *"After learning of all the business that goes with business, I'm a little intimidated, but figure that other people have made it through all of this and I will figure it out as well."*

If this is you, then by all means get started!

Scenario 3: *"After learning of all the business that goes with business, I'm not worried, and do not care to even think about the issues that may exist."*

Hold on, you might not have enough paranoia to survive in business. I have nothing to tell you except to be careful.

"I haven't saved enough money to start."
Conventional wisdom says that to start a business requires a lot of money and that a smart person will work as an employee for someone else while setting aside funds until he can afford to start his business.

While this is admirable, I find it nearly impossible in today's environment. There are few jobs/wages and lifestyles that allow sufficient funding to really make a difference in the financing of a business. Do not despair; the good news is that it has never been easier to a) operate a business with very little money (excluding your compensation), and b) with certain types of businesses, obtain outside funding. If you are willing to give up some television and socializing time, it is absolutely possible to run a business on the side while still working at your job. This is not easy or at all glamorous, but it requires very little investment and can be a great first step to your ultimate dream.

The other option is to raise funds from an investor or lender. As I write this, the funding environment is strong and obtaining capital is relatively easy for a decent idea and a strong pitch. There are personal credit cards, traditional banks, a variety of next-generation online lenders, angel investors seemingly everywhere, and venture capital. Educate yourself on these various methods. They all have pros and cons and there are many resources in books and online to provide information on these potential sources of funding.

Scenario 1: *"I am not comfortable with debt, and my business is not sexy enough for an investor."*

If you are willing to work hard, I suggest getting started while simultaneously earning a living as an employee full- or part-time. However, don't waste your time on this if you don't have a clear plan to get 100 percent to your business. Without a clear plan to get away from the job that is essentially providing your startup capital, it is easy to get stuck doing both, which will not ultimately get you to your dream.

Scenario 2: *"I am willing to do anything to start on my dream. I'll use my personal credit. I'll guarantee loans. I'll give up a piece of what will someday be incredibly valuable so I can get started."*

You need to drop what you are doing and start executing on your business immediately. The more of your time and energy going towards it the better. Try to give it 100 percent if at all possible.

Scenario 3: *"I am passionate about my business but not comfortable with debt, and I am not willing to work two jobs. My family needs me to support our current lifestyle, but I have to scratch this itch."*

You are in a tough but amazing spot. It is awesome to be sure you need to scratch the itch; it is tough when you need to support a decent quality of life and not assume debt while doing so.

You need to develop a quality plan and also prove out the concept as you can (demo, website, minimum viable product, etc). Ultimately you need to raise funds from an investor who believes in what you are doing enough to fund the costs of the business and pay you. This happens all of the time, so do not worry, but it will require you to be smart and good. You will likely also have to be very persistent.

In the end, if the itch is strong enough, a lack of personal funds should not stand in the way of getting started.

Eighty percent of businesses fail, and that is scary.
Many, perhaps most, businesses do fail. Failure is a little scary. We are blessed to live in a country that is quite forgiving of failure, but regardless, humans prefer to succeed, and failure hurts our psyche.

While I will not argue with the statistics, I do have a theory on this high failure rate. I presume that many failed businesses are started by people who had the external itch to start, but when they experienced the challenges of owning a business, they made the wise decision that their quality of life would be better without it. This is not to say that starting a business is easy and will succeed if you have the internal itch. However, I am confident that among people with an internal itch and a high degree of persistence, the failure rate is much lower than the published numbers.

Regardless, there is a chance your business will fail. What will you do?

Scenario 1: *"Failing would embarrass me and disappoint my family and friends, which would bother me."*

You may not want to start. I am a strong believer that what you fear and think about, you somehow steer towards, and a strong fear of failure may actually lead you toward it.

Scenario 2: *"Failure would be awful. I will work hard and use everything at my disposal to succeed. However, if I fail, I will know that I gave it everything I had and take it as a learning experience. I prefer to risk it all chasing success rather than let the risk of failure get in my way."*

You should pursue the business. Failure is less likely if you are not seriously afraid of it. Chasing success is the key to achieving it. There is always risk. As long as your life will not significantly suffer if you fail, you are ready for this journey.

Scenario 3: *"Failure is a badge of honor; I welcome it.*

You are someone I truly do not understand. The glorification of failure is abhorrent to me. While failure can be a great teacher and ultimately lead to greater success, you should not welcome it, but avoid it.

I know I want to start a business, but I don't know what business to start. Having the perfect/unique idea to pour everything into is an elusive thing. I believe the chance at success is exponentially better when you do something you have a natural interest in, and the stronger the interest the better. (How lame am I that my thing was accounting?)

Scenario 1:" *I have a great, unique idea that is in an area I have been interested in since my youth."*

Do it! You have that elusive match of interest and feasible business idea. Try it; even if you fail you will enjoy the journey. Your risk of failure is much less if you truly have this match. When the passion for what you are doing is there, a way to success is usually forged. However, it will likely still require a significant amount of effort. One's ability to put forth that effort and not quit is strongest when there is passion for the idea beyond wealth and fear of failure. If this is you, get started on your business now.

Scenario 2: *"I am convinced that owning a business is what I need to do. As soon as that great idea hits me, I will start it and drop everything to make it succeed."*

This is a tough spot. I was there for several years. My advice is to just start. Did I mention I like action? Do something! It will likely not be your "it" business, but it will take you toward your "it" business. For me it was telecommunications > real estate > CPA firm > refrigeration > healthcare > cloud reporting and bookkeeping (final destination, my "it"). I kept doing things (some on the side and others full-time) to chase my "it" business. It was not efficient, it was not economical, and it was far from easy. But it led me to where I am, and I could not be happier. I am not sure my mind would have developed the "it" idea without this rambling journey. So my advice -- granted it's a little biased -- is to act. It is possible that this journey will ultimately become the guide to your "it" business.

Scenario 3: "*I think I want to start a business, but I don't want to do it for the business itself. I want that perfect idea that is me before I start.*"

You are in a good spot. My only advice is to search for that idea. Don't just talk about it. Research, learn, and discover what it is. Simply be sure that if you truly want the perfect business to start, you will still need to make it happen; it rarely falls out of the sky.

In summary

Starting a business can be very attractive. However, there are a multitude of reasons not to do so. I started a business that I am passionate about, and I could not be happier. If your desire to start a business is an internal itch, then there is little that should stop you. The "why nots" should now apply only to how you go about starting.

Chapter Six

Why haven't you traveled the world?

Courtney Derr

It was 2013, and I was your typical young professional in a respectable 9-to-5 desk job. I was climbing the professional ladder and happily married, the "perfect" picture completed by a dashing dachshund and cute little Washington, DC row house. My husband, H.J., and I should have been saving for a house and talking about growing our family.

Instead, we quit our jobs, put everything into storage, and left our home for a year-long journey, motorcycling through Southeast Asia and beyond in search of adventure, personal fulfillment, and good eats.

What the hell, right?

If you have that reaction, you're not alone. While the majority of people in our lives were supportive, many even jealous, some just did not get it:

- "Why would you give up good careers? You're fatally interrupting your prime earning years."
- "Why Asia? You've never even been there."
- "Why now? You're too old for this foolishness."
- "Why motorcycles? Are you crazy?"

Why, why, why, why, why. In retrospect we should have expected such questions, but they surprised us at the time.

As this book suggests, our response to all that was to shrug and say: "Why not?"

To most people in our lives, our world trip came out of nowhere -- a ripple in the space-time continuum of our humdrum lives.

But really, the story of this journey starts way back in 2007 with the story of us.

H.J. and I were introduced by a mutual friend at a bar in DC on May 2, 2007. Despite the many beers consumed that evening, we know the exact date because I still have the business card he gave me that night with the date scribbled on the back.

Neither of us was looking for a relationship. I was 22 and had just come off of a string of bad dating experiences. H.J. was 27 and saving up for a life of George Clooney-style bachelordom.

It started out casually enough. We'd run into each other at work events and exchange flirty emails. After a couple of weeks of this back and forth, he showed up sans wingman to my 23rd birthday party – impressive, right?

About a month later, he invited me home to meet his family (at their 35th wedding anniversary party, no less) – three months later, he met mine, and it wasn't long before we were planning our first trip together.

"Normal" people might go to NYC or a little countryside B&B for the weekend … you know, ease into things as a new couple. Candlelight, fancy meals, roses, bubble baths – all fairytale romance stuff.

We decided to rent a house on the Osa Peninsula in Costa Rica. Though Costa Rica is now firmly a holiday hot spot, tourism was, at best, still in its infancy in Osa in 2007.

We watched all the other tourists hop on planes bound for beach resort towns like Quepos and Tamarindo while we waited with exactly one other passenger going our way – a Peace Corps volunteer working on a turtle conservation project.

Our weekend in Osa went something like this: bumpy rides down muddy "roads" better suited to ATVs; rain; no Wi-Fi; more rain; no phone; even more rain; *zero* open restaurants; and more rain. There was nothing to do except hang out with all manner of bugs, several species of monkey, and other jungle critters taking refuge from the rain in our open-air *casa*. Flights were canceled, and we ended up getting stuck for days on account of, you guessed it, rain.

What might have been a miserable trip for some was an awesome adventure for us. That trip pretty much sealed the deal: we were engaged less than a year later.

After we got married in 2009, our desire to travel intensified. We honeymooned in Nicaragua, frequented Paris, road-tripped to Maine, tackled Alaska and British Columbia, and survived a canoe trip with our dachshund on the James River in Virginia that landed H.J. in the hospital (long story for another time).

Like so many people, our trips were the highlights of each year, and they were never long or frequent enough. The list of things we wanted to see and do was expanding exponentially as the years flew by.

Along with this wanderlust was a rapidly growing sense that DC was not the place for us. Don't get me wrong – it's an exciting and beautiful city that boasts great food, museums, and nightlife. We made some amazing friends there. But, in our hearts, we just couldn't connect with the fast-paced, ambitious-at-all-costs vibe. We were less than enamored of our career paths, and we longed for life in a smaller, more affordable, friendlier place. If it offered outdoor attractions, all the better.

We began to look in earnest for jobs elsewhere in 2010. We applied to jobs in places like Montana, New Hampshire, and Georgia. Hell, we even looked for jobs overseas. We searched far and wide in familiar sectors (at the time, we both had strong ties to the political world) and those brand new to us.

As it turned out, the job market post-recession was pretty tough in all but the richest of places, and thanks to crony capitalism, DC was just about the richest. Stuck we were for the time being.

As all this was going down, we both independently stumbled across the concept of the modern nomad: folks like us who were well into (less than satisfying) careers, wondering if this was really it in life. Unlike us, these intrepid souls looked at that life (professional drudgery, mortgage, kids, the works), said "Screw it," and hit the open road.

We were green with envy. We had a million reasons why we wanted to travel, but we immediately ran into our first answer to the "why not" question: money.

We had just gotten married, and our combined pre-marriage financial baggage plus an expensive engagement ring and some vacations we couldn't afford totaled nearly $35,000. Obviously, we weren't going anywhere soon with that hanging over our heads.

After allowing ourselves to wallow a tad too long in our jealousy of the nomads already on their journeys, we decided to put that emotion to positive use and get serious about paying down our debt.

We committed to paying a certain amount off at the beginning of every single month, no matter what. We also put every cent left over at the end of each month toward our debt.

To do so, we shed all unnecessary expenses, including gym memberships, evenings out, and expensive vacations. We sold H.J.'s car and became a one-car family. We weren't shoppers anyway, but we didn't buy anything unless we absolutely needed it. We rode our bikes everywhere we could (with a bonus of exercise and enjoyment!). We brought our lunches to work, and H.J. bought a coffee pot for his office instead of buying coffee every morning.

You'd be surprised how quickly that stuff adds up. Forgoing the Metro and the car saved us about $2,000/year alone. Opting out of the daily venti vanilla lattes netted us another $1500/year. Think about it – that's $7,000 in just two years and $14,000, or almost half our debt, in four.

All told, it took us about 20 months to pay off our debt, and I'm not going to lie – it sucked. Don't get me wrong: it felt amazing to see the downward trend, but to send that much money out the door and receive nothing in return was painful.

LESSON # 1: If you want to travel, get rid of your debt. Get rid of your debt, period. It's not worth it.

Our debt cleared, we could finally begin saving. Boy did it feel glorious to see the green line in our bank account rise for the first time ever. We began to plan for our trip in earnest.

Inspired by actor Ewan McGregor's epic round-the-world journey documented in the film *Long Way Round*, we decided that motorcycling would be an awesome way for us to see the world. Enter "why not" number two: I had no idea how to ride a motorcycle.

We set about tackling this next roadblock by enrolling in a motorcycle safety course in nearby Charlottesville, VA. Our hope was that this first step would answer the question of whether we even enjoyed riding motorcycles.

For H.J., it was an immediate yes. Me, not so much.

Not having a mechanical background or even experience driving a manual-transmission in a car, I struggled for the first few hours of the class to get a feel for the machine. I stalled over and over again, and there may have been a few tears of anger and frustration. But eventually something clicked, and once I got it we never looked back.

I was hooked despite a nasty skid that left my clothes torn and took off a few layers of skin. We passed the class, got our motorcycle licenses, and bought "starter" bikes just a few weeks later.

LESSON # 2: Don't be afraid to push yourself and try new things – being challenged is how personal growth happens, and you might just surprise yourself. At the very worst, you'll know more about your own preferences.

We spent the next year saving and riding around the DC area, practicing as much as possible. H.J. graduated from the starter bike to a BMW 650 dual-sport – it was meant to be the bike he'd take around the world.

Then a series of financial misfortunes befell us, notably two years of erroneously withholding too little for income taxes. Yes, we made the same mistake twice, and it put a sizable dent in our savings. (Note: we no longer do our own taxes.)

We also took a good hard look at our trip budget and realized we were significantly underestimating the costs. We'd need to save $40k more than we initially planned.

What was once a two-and-half-year preparation period suddenly became five, and given that we wanted kids and I was rapidly approaching 30, it began to feel too unrealistic. We had a million answers to the "Why not?" question, it seemed.

We abandoned the dream.

Looking back, I have no idea why that seemed like the only solution. We could have altered plans, abandoned the motorcycle idea, looked at a shorter time frame – there were a million ways we could have pivoted and adapted our plans, but we didn't.

There we were in 2012 – still stuck in DC.

I was enjoying my career more by that the time, but H.J. was still very much unfulfilled. We decided to use some of the money we saved to send him to a professional videography/filmmaking certification program through Boston University. (He's a passionate photographer.) We hoped he could build a portfolio and enough business to eventually go full-time.

The program turned out to be a bust, and he withdrew a few months after he started. Thankfully, we got most of our money back, and his early departure turned out to be a blessing -- the school shut its doors just a few months later, leaving the remaining students out all the money they paid.

That it was a blessing did not soften the blow for my husband. He was making decent money at his full-time job and genuinely liked most of his colleagues, but it wasn't enough. He absolutely hated the work (politics) and the old-school office culture, one that required his butt to be parked in front of a computer from 9 to 5, wearing a tie even if he had no meetings because … otherwise you're not working.

He wanted out desperately but was struggling to find a path forward.

Though I enjoyed my job, it wasn't enough to make up for that, and the full weight of it hit me one morning.

It was a Sunday in March 2013, and we were lazing about in bed when I turned to him and said: "So we don't have enough money to do the trip we wanted, but what kind of trip *could* we do with what we have?"

He responded right away: "Southeast Asia – we could live like kings for a year or more, easily, with what we have saved."

I said: "Let's do it."

Seriously, just like that, whatever it was that was holding us back in 2012 about the money, timing, etc. -- it just vanished.

LESSON # 3: Things change, and it's never too late or early to pursue your dream. Oh, and if you're waiting for the exact right time, you'll be waiting forever.

We left the US roughly nine months later and arrived in Ho Chi Minh City on November 20, 2013. We bought motorcycles with the plan to ride them all the way through Vietnam, Laos, Cambodia, Thailand, Malaysia, and hopefully beyond – India, Myanmar, perhaps even putting them on a boat to Indonesia.

We made it a little less than halfway through that plan.

After a rocky start for me in southern Vietnam (I totally underestimated how difficult riding conditions in Asia would be), we were finally getting into the swing of things and starting to relish our time on the road when our junky $300 bikes started revolting.

By the time we reached the world-famous caves of central Vietnam, mechanical problems that had cropped up once a week or so turned into an almost daily occurrence, and many of these were beyond our expertise (e.g., electrical issues). All of a sudden the majority of our time was consumed by these problems and the consequent rearranging of our plans instead of riding. Not exactly how we envisioned the trip.

We decided to invest big money on full tune-ups for our bikes and ship them to Hanoi for a fresh start on our journey north. It cost us $50, which sounds laughably low now that we're back in the US, but that is a *lot* of money in Vietnam.

On reaching Hanoi, we put in an application for visa extensions, which would take nearly three weeks to receive, thanks to general government red tape and the Tet holiday. (Virtually the entire country shuts down for at least a few days – the government was closed for over 10 days.)

We decided to kill some time while waiting for our visa extensions by taking our good-as-new (ha!) bikes on a little jaunt to the famous karsts of Halong Bay. Just a few hours into our ride, H.J.'s bike up and died.

We were in the middle of nowhere – no hotels around and no businesses even open, thanks to the holiday. Right then and there, we knew we were done with those bikes.

I won't bore you with the details of our epic struggle to get the bike running again – it's enough to know that we did and were able to limp back to Hanoi.

Despite all this, we were still determined to see our bike adventure through. We sold our junkers and bought factory-new Honda dual-sports guaranteed to run, cross international borders, and handle the mountains of Vietnam's famed Ha Giang province.

We left Hanoi on February 22 feeling renewed and invigorated despite the drizzly cold weather. Our new bikes could hit 100 kph and roll over bumps like it was nothing!

Our enthusiasm was dulled as the day wore on and the rain continued. By the time we arrived at our destination, we were soaked through to our underwear. We ended up staying an extra day just to allow our clothes and shoes to dry.

This happened for a week straight. We bought new rubber boots, which all the local farmers use, to keep our feet dry. We bought big furry mitts that fit over the handlebars to keep my hands warm. We tried everything we could, but it was still no use. We just could not keep the rain out, and it went on like this for three more weeks, a few sunny days notwithstanding.

The north of Vietnam is known for its otherworldly and rugged mountain terrain, one that few tourists see, and the few times the rain abated and the clouds lifted, we were left in awe of the landscape. But, for the most part, we'd ride from destination to destination, arrive soaked to our underwear, and then spend the next day or two waiting for our clothes to dry out before repeating.

It's hard to describe how exhausting and demoralizing this was. We spent so long saving for and dreaming about this trip, and that dream did not involving sitting on a motorcycle in freezing cold rain, soaking wet and shivering for days on end, nary a view to enjoy.

LESSON # 4: Sometimes your dreams aren't all you thought they would be.

Other things also started to change during this time. Food options dwindled to nothing. Most of the towns we stayed in had very few restaurants – maybe a soup cart (generally open only in the mornings), a sandwich cart or two (again, open only in the morning), some ladies grilling hot dogs street side, and an uncomfortable number of dog and/or cat establishments (not kidding). We spent our fair share of nights eating aforementioned hot dogs and chips in our room.

The town of Tra Linh was particularly inhospitable – after being inexplicably turned away from three restaurants that were clearly serving customers, we ended up eating chao (porridge) with meat that was not familiar-tasting. Best-case scenario is horse meat, and sadly, I'm pretty sure it wasn't. Suffice it to say it was not exactly the culinary adventure we were hoping for.

Then there was the cultural shift. Northern Vietnam is decidedly less friendly than the south, and many people were downright hostile to us as foreigners. It's not entirely surprising – the area is home to various hill tribes, notorious for being insular societies, as well as other ethnic minorities, hardened by years of conflict with both Laos and China. (Violence between Vietnam and the latter is still going on.)

That it is understandable didn't make it any easier to deal with at the time. For example, what do you do when you find a 14-year old girl sitting on your brand-new $3,000 motorcycle without permission, giggling? If she drops the bike and damages it, I'm sure she will be sorry, but can she (or her family) afford to fix it? Could you ask that of someone who has so little when you have so much? Can you even explain this to her without sounding like an asshole? Will she understand since she barely speaks English? Are you even in the right to be angry since she doesn't mean any harm by it?

What do you do when you are in the middle of nowhere and a mechanic charges you over $10 to fix a flat tire, when the going rate in Vietnam is around $1; when a taxi driver tells you a rate and then demands double when you arrive at your destination, threatening to call the police if you don't pay; when a hotel manager promises you safe parking inside the hotel for your motorcycle, only to renege on that promise after you have already paid and unpacked? Or when you try to get your laptop fixed, and the shop sends it to Hanoi without your permission, telling you it will cost triple to repair and take three days as opposed to the one day promised?

We dealt with each of these situations and more.

This is not to say that we quit because we had some bad food and people were mean to us. That's just silly. But this period did prompt us to seriously examine our expectations and priorities on this trip. With a limited and dwindling amount of savings and thus time, we had to ask ourselves if how we were spending both was worth it.

LESSON # 5: Learning when to call it quits is one of the hardest and most important things a person can learn in life.

Ultimately, we ended up riding through Laos and loving it (easily our favorite country in SE Asia – go now!) as well northeastern Thailand, ending our motorcycle journey in Siem Reap, Cambodia. We sold our bikes there after five months of riding.

It ended up being a bittersweet parting – though we were sad to leave our bikes behind, not being tied down opened up a whole world, literally, of possibilities.

We met up with my parents in Thailand, explored Chiang Mai and the mountains of the north, dove on the island of Koh Tao, and hit up Penang, Malaysia, before finally saying goodbye in Singapore.

By then it was summer, and we were in need of beach R&R. We spent a month doing exactly that in Indonesia. From there it was onto Sri Lanka and India. We loved Sri Lanka, but India was another story – a story for another day lest you think our entire trip was one horrible experience.

We then hopped to Oman, experiencing a small but important part of the Middle East, before finishing with a road trip through Europe that broadened our waistlines, drained our bank account, and reinvigorated our spirits.

We flew home on November 19, 2014 – exactly 365 days after we left.

When we set out on this journey, we had no idea what the future held for us. We thought there was a distinct possibility that we would never come back – either we would figure out how to make enough money off of our blog to travel indefinitely, or we would find a place that suited us better than America.

In a twist that shocked the hell out of us, it turns out that the US suits us quite nicely, and unlike a lot of other nomads, our entry back into our home culture was quite easy. I even accepted a job offer from my previous employer.

One thing that did change: we managed to get out of DC. *Finally.* It only took a year of travel and tens of thousands of dollars to do it. Hey, there are worse ways it could have happened.

We settled in Portland, OR, where I work remotely at a 9-5 desk job. And you know what? I don't hate it. I actually quite like it. H.J. has not returned to the 9-5 life and is working to build a photography business. We live a pretty quiet life that involves spending a lot of time at home and enjoying the outdoors – a life not very different than the one we left behind in 2013. And we're totally ok with that.

We still get the "why?" question. Quite often. And when I'm not feeling contrarian enough to parry back with a "Why not?," I answer with a paraphrase of the following quote:

> Average people around you will sacrifice every principle and every truth for the sake of security. People, with very few exceptions, fear the uncertainty of an unknown future more than the seeming security of a known status quo. They will give up every right and every bit of their souls for the promise of security.... You can break free of this tendency, but it takes courage, risk-taking, and a conscious act of defying convention.

--Jeffrey Tucker, *Advice for Young, Unemployed Workers* (and a contributor to this book!)

This quote so perfectly captures the essence of "why not?" by laying bare the assumptions behind the "why?" Things change: industries evolve, companies go under or get sold, leaders come and go. And people change: they get sick, they discover religion or shed their faith, they fall in or out of love, they discover a new passion.

To assume safety in the status quo is to misunderstand (and reject) the nature of existence.

I'll close by posing a final question to you – one that we posed to ourselves when we first conceived of this journey: "what if ...?"

This is, to me, far more important than the "why?" or the "why not?" "What if..." dares you to dream, to imagine the possibilities before you, and to take that chance.

We'll never sit in our rocking chairs one day, old and gray, wondering how our lives would have been different if we had pursued our dreams to travel. We *know* how they're different. And that is the most valuable lesson of all.

So go ahead and ask yourself: what if I pursued *my* dream?

Chapter Seven

Why haven't you auditioned for American Idol?

TK Coleman

Music has always been my first love. I grew up in a religious home where gospel music was played all throughout the day. From Walter Hawkins and James Moore to Commissioned, Take 6, and The Winans Brothers, there was hardly ever a moment when my brothers and I weren't trying to emulate the vocal stylings of our favorite singers. At the church where we grew up it was common for all the young boys to form singing quartets. Nothing was cooler than being a guy who knew how to sing.

When I started high school I discovered Brian McKnight and Boyz II Men. I listened to their CDs over and over again trying to master every note as if my life depended on it. Sometimes I would spend hours trying to hit the high notes at the end of "On Bended Knee" from Boyz II Men's second album. I even remember staying up late every night to watch Jay Leno and Arsenio Hall just in case Brian McKnight or Boyz II Men made an appearance. I loved their music so much that I couldn't imagine a life doing anything but writing songs that moved people in the same way their music moved me. When I went to college my dorm mates nicknamed me "singing boy" because I would always hang out by the hallway staircase, where the acoustics were amazing, practicing my notes. Music was my life.

Paradoxically, I never majored in music. I was too scared. Auditions for the music department required you to prepare a classical song in a foreign language. I had neither the confidence nor the work ethic to pull that off. In all honesty I wasn't that great of a singer outside the realm of pop and R&B. Had the music department allowed me to audition with a Boyz II Men piece, I would've been first in line. Instead of music I chose to major in theatre (my second love) and philosophy (a field I ended up discovering as a result of all the confusion I constantly felt about following my dreams and living a meaningful life). I never stopped singing though. From the shower and the dorm hallway to talent shows and long walks across campus, I sang passionately every single day.

I even remember one occasion when I visited the student loan office and the lady who was working commented on how happy I seemed. This struck me as a peculiar observation because I was particularly sad that day. But then I realized: "I'm singing. She thinks I'm happy because I'm singing." That moment actually cheered me up. It made me smile because it illustrated something I've always believe about the power of music: there is something inherently courageous and joyful about the act of singing a song. My love for singing pulled me through a lot of dark days and boring classes.

Why haven't you auditioned for American Idol?

"American Idol auditions are in Detroit next week. You have to go, man. You have to go. Nobody loves to sing like you do."

Those were words spoken to me via telephone by my friend Page Kennedy. Page was a theatre major from Western Michigan University and was living in Los Angeles at the time. He is one of the few people I know who studied theatre and is now making a living as a professional actor. He's had roles on *Weeds*, *Backstrom*, *Blue Mountain State*, *SWAT*, and many other TV shows and movies. Page is an accomplished guy, an inspiration for a lot of aspiring artists who come from the Midwest. So when he called me from LA to tell me that he thought I should audition for *American Idol*, I was truly flattered.

"TK, this show is perfect for you. Everyone knows how much you love to sing. If the judges on the show were able to see your passion and hear your voice, I believe you'd become a star."

I told him I was honored by his belief in my talents, but that I wasn't interested in doing that audition. I had already made peace with the fact that I would probably not have a career in music, and I was really beginning to feel at home in the philosophy department. Auditioning for *American Idol* seemed like a pipe dream, an untimely distraction, and a not-so enviable opportunity to be embarrassed by Simon Cowell. I was partly scared of the idea and partly trying to focus my mind along more pragmatic lines. To audition for *American Idol* might not only lead to failure, but it also might cause me to open my heart so wide that I'd never be able to recover from the heartbreak of getting my hopes up and losing. I gave Page a firm "no" and ended the conversation.

One week went by. Page Kennedy called me again.

"T.K., there's another *American Idol* audition coming up in California. You have to go, man. I know you're scared, but you have to go after your passion, man. Imagine the possibilities."

I laughed at his persistence, but I maintained my original position. That's when Page upped the ante: "I will pay for you to fly out here. That's how passionate I am about you doing this."

Page was one of those guys who understood the possibility of going after a crazy dream and somehow making it happen. If there was anyone who not only talked the talk, but who actually walked the walk, it was Page. "Auditioning for *American Idol* couldn't be any more far-fetched than Page's decision to move to Hollywood and make his dreams come true," I reasoned. I told Page to give me some time and promised him I would think about it.

Since I had good relationships and a tremendous amount of respect for my professors, I asked many of them for their opinion. None of them were impressed by the idea. The fact that I would need to miss a few classes didn't help. I wouldn't categorize any of my professors as dream killers. I think they were all well-meaning people who just wanted to see me stay focused. But I have to admit that I was more than a bit discouraged by the general lack of enthusiasm over Page's suggestion.

There was one professor in the philosophy department, however, who provided a different take on things. Her name was Sylvia Culp. I had never taken any classes with her before, so we didn't have much of a relationship. I only asked for her opinion because she happened to be sitting in her office one day when I was walking by. This was a rare thing in my experience. Prior to that moment, I was mostly accustomed to seeing her door closed. I interpreted her open door as a sign of some sort, an invitation from the universe to seek out a different opinion. I also think I was looking for someone who would tell me what I wanted to hear.

I asked her for some time, and she was very gracious as she listened to me talk about this crazy idea Page had about my auditioning for *American Idol*. After listening very intently, she said, "This world has enough philosophers who don't anything about following their dreams and taking creative risks. If you plan on teaching some day, you better have some wisdom from substantial real-world experiences to impart. The best philosophers are the people who live passionate lives. The opportunity to do philosophy isn't going to go away. You can do that at any age. But something like this only comes around every once in a while. Once you start to get older it's only going to get easier to talk yourself out of things like this. Go get yours answers, young man. Go get your questions answered, or you're going to torture yourself with regret." Those words were exactly what I needed to hear.

Later that night I called Page and told him I would accept his offer. He was excited. After that talk with Sylvia Culp, I was starting to feel the magic again. I could hear the music calling me home.

Why haven't you auditioned for American Idol?

I didn't have much time to prepare for my audition, so I asked one of my philosophy buddies if he had any suggestions. He said, "If you want to prepare for *American Idol*, you have to master your nerves. It doesn't matter how much you practice in the shower or in the hallways. You need to practice singing in scary situations."

"Like what?" I asked.

"You need to walk around campus and stop random people on their way to class. I mean, total strangers. Tell them you're planning on auditioning for *American Idol* and that you'd like to get their feedback on your singing. That's scary as hell. If you can do something crazy and embarrassing like that, you'll definitely be ready for the real deal."

I accepted his challenge. For the next two days I was a man on a mission. A friend and I went out to conduct this crazy experiment. "Start with the girls," my friend said. "They love that kind of stuff."

"Excuse me," I said to a girl walking by. "I'm planning on auditioning for *American Idol*, and I'm just going around campus asking random people if I can sing for them as way to practice for the show. Can I sing for you?"

"I'm sure you'll do just fine," she said as she kept going.

My friend laughed and said, "Don't worry. She probably thought you were trying to flirt with her. Think about it. It totally sounds like a pick-up line. Okay, let's try asking some guys first."

We saw three guys walking our way, and my friend said to try them. I approached the guys and repeated the same line I had said to the girl. The guys looked at each other as if they were thinking, "Is this dude serious?" Then one of them said, "Go ahead, man." I sang the first verse of "Please Don't Go Away" by Boyz II Men. When I finished, they all laughed. But this wasn't a mocking kind of laugh. It was the kind of laugh one does when he's proud, pleasantly surprised, or impressed. All three guys stepped forward to shake my hand. "I won't lie," said one of the guys. "When you first asked us if you could sing, I thought you were going to be wack. But you've got some skill, bro. Do your thing, man."

From that moment on I felt increasingly empowered. I sang for anyone who would listen. I sang for girls and guys alike without fear. On the day before I flew to California I walked into a campus coffee shop, stood on a chair, and asked everyone for their attention. I said, "I know this sounds crazy, but what I'm about to tell you is true. Tomorrow I get on a plane to fly to California for an *American Idol* audition. I would like to sing for you all as a last-minute attempt to prepare for the madness." Before I could hit a single note, everyone applauded.

To them it didn't matter if I sounded good or not. They were impressed that someone would do something as crazy as walk into a coffee shop and do what I did. When I finished singing, everyone who wasn't already standing got up from their seats and showed me love like I never had received it before. At that moment I realized something I would never forget: the mere fact that I was following a dream was big enough to make the people around me feel like they were a part of something magical and meaningful. I've always wanted to inspire people, but until that moment I had always assumed that I would need to be successful or famous before I could light a fire inside someone else's heart. That experience taught me differently. I knew when I got on that plane that something more than my personal dream was at stake: I was on a mission to show everyone by example that it was okay to step outside his or her comfort zone in order to reach for something spectacular.

When my feet stepped on California ground, I felt as though the energy of the stars was with me. I knew in my gut that something special was about to happen. The audition process was different from what I had watched on TV. I was told to get there the night before because people would be camping outside. I did as I was instructed, and several hundred people were already in line at 10 p.m. I remember staying up until 2 a.m. talking with aspiring singers from around the country.

While exchanging stories, dreams, and lessons learned with the people around me, I could hear lots of people practicing their audition songs. It was a surreal experience. For the first time in my life I slept on the streets. In the morning someone announced that we each needed a ticket to audition, but no one was guaranteed a ticket. We stood in that line for a full day and finally received tickets. I was told that many people who showed up later than we did would not get one. For the rest of that night I held on to my ticket as if it were made of pure gold. "Sweet dreams. sweeter manifestations" was the mantra I chanted to myself as I drifted off to sleep that night.

The next day was showtime. As we were ushered into the arena, I was mesmerized by the sheer number of people. The stands were filled as if it were Game 7 of an NBA Finals match. When I walked to the bathroom at one point, all I could hear was the sounds of people belting out their songs without shame. I walked past a girl who made eye contact and said, "You ready?" I said, "Yeah, you ready?" She said, "Yep. Here you go." And she started to sing her song right there. Then she asked me to go. I sang my song right there. Then she looked at me and said, "Respect." I said, "Respect," and that was that. For the first time in my life I felt like I was home among fellow dreamers. We were all a bunch of crazy misfits trying to achieve crazy things. I knew I wanted to feel that kind of energy for the rest of my life.

Four parallel tables stood on the arena floor, with three people -- the producers -- at each. The people auditioning sat in the stands, divided into groups of 20. When a group was summoned, the members would stand in front of a table. The producers at each table called forward the first four people from their group and, moving left to right, asked each person to sing. After about 30-60 seconds the person singing would be asked to stop and the next person in line would begin his or her song. After the four finished the producers told them to enter through the door on their right or exit through the door on their left. Being invited to enter on the right meant you advanced to the next round of the auditioning process. Being directed to the door on the left meant you were done.

My heart stopped several times as I saw many great singers exit via the door on the left. When my time came, I was ready for my moment of destiny. I stepped up and sang "Back at One" by Brian McKnight. When my group was done, the producers directed me to the door on the left. I couldn't believe it. Everything I did to prepare for that moment felt so right. It truly seemed as if this was all meant to be. And in a flash, I was done. The dramatic phone conversations with Page, the inspiring speech from Sylvia Culp, the epic moment when I sang for everyone in the coffee shop, sleeping outside for a ticket to audition: it all came to a head in less than a few undramatic minutes. Being the next American Idol was not in my cards.

It sure didn't feel like it at the moment, but this is one of the best experiences I ever had. At this point in my story you're probably expecting to hear some lesson on the value of failure and how setbacks are the key to success. While I'm definitely an advocate of such an idea, that's not the main lesson I took away from my *American Idol* experience. Before that audition I believed that the primary purpose for following one's dreams was to actually achieve them. I've always been motivated by people who set out to do great things and who defied all the odds on their path to extraordinary achievement. As amazing and inspiring as such stories are, they often seduce us into missing what I take to be the real value in chasing a dream or pursuing something extraordinary.

Following your heart is not only a creative journey of going after what you want, it is also an evolutionary journey of becoming who you really are. It's impossible to pursue a dream while remaining the same person you were when you first conceived the dream. When you move in the direction of your dreams, you initiate an alchemical process that results in radical personal transformation. The challenges you'll have to overcome, the fears you'll need to face, the mistakes you'll make, the ecstatic moments you'll experience, the people you'll meet—these will all be triggers activating aspects of your soul that you never knew existed.

I believe that the true source of a meaningful, fulfilling, and adventurous life is self-knowledge and self-actualization. W. E. B. Du Bois wrote, "The most important thing to remember is this: to be ready at any moment to give up what you are for what you might become." Each of us has a possible self that can neither be understood nor unearthed from within our comfort zones. The version of you that tries something daring and fails is superior, in every way, to the version of you that doesn't try at all. The main purpose of a goal is not the goal itself, but the movement towards self-knowledge and self-actualization, which it inspires. There is no distinction between the taking of a creative risk and the decision to consciously participate in one's own evolution.

Some people look at my audition experience as a failure. I agree. Positive thinking aside, I failed to accomplish what I set out to accomplish. What comforts me is not some warm and fuzzy belief about how failure isn't really failure, but the experiential understanding I have of the fact that failure is less intimidating and more nourishing when you experience it from the inside out. Failure is horrifying when you contemplate it as an idea. When you taste failure as an experience, however, you get to see what you're made of in an entirely unique way.

I talk to people all the time who want to do things that are daring and different, but they're looking for some kind of assurance that they'll succeed.

I'm here to tell you the opposite. If you follow your dreams, you'll probably suffer some losses and heartbreaks that you can't even imagine. But you'll also realize that you're funnier, wiser, more courageous, more interesting, more creative, more resilient, more confident, and more influential than you can even imagine.

My present-day career is completely unrelated to my childhood music dreams. Yet few things have prepared me for my career and my life more than my *American Idol* experience. Whenever I need to dig deep into my soul for answers, encouragement, or guidance, I thank my younger self for providing me with such a rich and bottomless well of stories that I can draw substance from.

If you want to be fascinating, do things that fascinate you. If you want to be inspiring, do things that inspire you. If you want to invoke ambition in others, demand great things of yourself. The world needs teachers, role models, philosophers, parents, and leaders who understand what it means to experience the personal transformation that comes from going after something special.

Like the yellow brick road of Oz, if you follow your dreams the path will take you on an adventure that is as frightening as it is thrilling. But when you "arrive," you'll discover that the real magic was inside your soul all along, and the road you traveled was simply one of self-discovery. Take a risk. Face your fears. Follow the yellow brick road. Success or not, the knowledge of your true self awaits. And that's far more valuable than anything else you can search for.

By the way, my *American Idol* experience eventually inspired me to move to California to pursue more of that creative energy I felt. In the first week after moving a woman stopped me at the shopping mall and started asking me all sorts of questions about who I was and what I was doing.

It turns out that she was a producer, and she wanted me to audition for a TV show called *Are You Smarter Than a 5th Grader?* She said to me, "You look like the kind of guy people would root for. You'd be great for that show." So I followed her tip and made the show. Yes, I actually met Jeff Foxworthy, and he's even cooler in person.

Unfortunately, I got the first question wrong. Fortunately, one of the kids saved me, and I was able to survive long enough to take home $50,000. I still failed though. At the end of the episode I had to look at the camera and say, "I'm T.K. Coleman, and I'm not smarter than a fifth grader."

I may not be smarter than a fifth grader, but I know a thing or two about taking chances, failing, discovering interesting things about my potential, and living to tell the story.

So as Sylvia Culp advised me, I advise you:

One day, all you'll have is your stories. So go live a life that makes an interesting and intoxicating story to tell. Why not?

Chapter Eight

Why haven't you had a bunch of kids?

Antony Davies[14]

Why not have a bunch of kids? My wife and I have many kids. We didn't plan to have many kids. It just sort of happened. After our fifth child was born, a friend asked my wife how many children she planned to have. She said, "Two."

How do you move them around?

Flying is out of the question unless you're willing to leave most of them at home or you can afford to buy a plane.

The number of vehicles that can fit your family is inversely proportional to the number of children you have. Where reasonable vehicles are concerned, the practical limit on family size is eight. For eight people, you'll find a grand total of maybe two options. Those two vehicles look the same, perform the same, and cost the same. You get to pick the color, but that's about the extent of your consumer choice. There are no vehicles for families with seven children. You have to jump straight to vehicles that will seat 15. It's as if car manufacturers have figured out that parents who cross the six-kid threshold are going to just keep pumping them out until their reproductive years peter out. So if you're going to make a vehicle that seats more than eight people, there's no point in designing it to fit anything less than 15.

With a lot of kids, divorce is less likely. As war buddies stick together through thick and thin, parents of large families stick together because of a shared combat experience. They don't have the luxury of disliking each other because they're already outnumbered in a field of complex and shifting alliances. Imagine dealing with midnight feedings, bed wetting, chicken pox, parent-teacher conferences, teenage angst, sketchy boyfriends, and overdue college tuition bills -- all within 24 hours. Repeatedly. Divorce isn't an option because you know that your partner will stick you with the kids.

How do you handle sickness?

Commercials where the kid has a cold and the parents give him cough syrup and lovingly tuck him into bed are a joke. Nursing numerous children is like playing whack-a-mole. One kid gets over his cold just in time for another to get it. No, they can't all be sick at once. They have to do it sequentially. What to a normal family would be a three-day cold, to a large family is a month-long affair. Other parents try to keep their children away from sick kids. Not you. When you have a lot of kids, you don't quarantine the sick ones. You want them to infect each other as quickly as possible because you need to process all of them before you come down with the bug yourself. You start

Why not have a bunch of kids? My wife and I have many kids. We didn't plan to have many kids. It just sort of happened. After our fifth child was born, a friend asked my wife how many children she planned to have. She said, "Two."

How do you move them around?

Flying is out of the question unless you're willing to leave most of them at home or you can afford to buy a plane.

The number of vehicles that can fit your family is inversely proportional to the number of children you have. Where reasonable vehicles are concerned, the practical limit on family size is eight. For eight people, you'll find a grand total of maybe two options. Those two vehicles look the same, perform the same, and cost the same. You get to pick the color, but that's about the extent of your consumer choice. There are no vehicles for families with seven children. You have to jump straight to vehicles that will seat 15. It's as if car manufacturers have figured out that parents who cross the six-kid threshold are going to just keep pumping them out until their reproductive years peter out. So if you're going to make a vehicle that seats more than eight people, there's no point in designing it to fit anything less than 15.

With a lot of kids, divorce is less likely. As war buddies stick together through thick and thin, parents of large families stick together because of a shared combat experience. They don't have the luxury of disliking each other because they're already outnumbered in a field of complex and shifting alliances. Imagine dealing with midnight feedings, bed wetting, chicken pox, parent-teacher conferences, teenage angst, sketchy boyfriends, and overdue college tuition bills -- all within 24 hours. Repeatedly. Divorce isn't an option because you know that your partner will stick you with the kids.

How do you handle sickness?

Commercials where the kid has a cold and the parents give him cough syrup and lovingly tuck him into bed are a joke. Nursing numerous children is like playing whack-a-mole. One kid gets over his cold just in time for another to get it. No, they can't all be sick at once. They have to do it sequentially. What to a normal family would be a three-day cold, to a large family is a month-long affair. Other parents try to keep their children away from sick kids. Not you. When you have a lot of kids, you don't quarantine the sick ones. You want them to infect each other as quickly as possible because you need to process all of them before you come down with the bug yourself. You start to thank God for the blessing of acquired immunity that guarantees each kid will only get the disease once.

Then you discover pink eye.

If dealing with a cold is like playing whack-a-mole, dealing with pink eye is like playing a macabre game of telephone. Kid #1 gives it to Kid #2, who gives it to Kid #3. By this time Kid #1 is cured, but Kid #3 has given it to Kid #4. Now Kid #1 has now forgotten your repeated warnings about washing his hands and keeping his fingers out of his brother's eye, and sure enough, Kid #1 has it again. He gives it to Kid #2, and the whole cycle continues. You find yourself praying for a harsh winter so the freezing temperatures can have a shot at killing off the germs that these house creatures have painted on to every surface.

What do you call them?

Names are a problem. We spent months selecting a name for our first child, Erika. We thought about how it sounded, what it meant, whether it had a long-enough shelf-life so it wouldn't make her sound like some old lady just as she was hitting her college years. Ladies named Mavis, Opal, Inez, and Violet weren't born 80-years-old. They just lost the shelf-life lottery. We were better at naming our second child, largely because I am a science-fiction freak and my hero, Isaac Asimov, had died just before our son was born. So Isaac it was. Our church friends thought it touching that we named him after the one of the biblical patriarchs. We didn't have the heart to admit that we named him after a lecherous chemistry professor who wrote wicked sci-fi.

After the first two, naming becomes easy. You already have a list of potentials in your head from previous research. You also have recyclable first-picks that you couldn't use because of gender issues. We knew that one of ours was going to be named Ivanka. Which one depended entirely on who showed up next with the appropriate plumbing.

By the time you get to #4 the months of researching and trying out different names and spelling variations gives way to grabbing the first name that doesn't rhyme with something crass so you can sign the paperwork and get out of the hospital. I figure that's why hospital employees all wear name tags. It's to give parents ideas. "OK, the baby gets the next name that comes down the hall. Wilbur. Crap. Well, that's the luck of the draw. Now sign those papers and let's get out of here before they find something else to charge us for."

Of course, with names come nicknames. At first, you're proud to tell people your baby's name. "She's Ivanka, after my wife's mother. Actually, there's been one Ivanka in each generation in my wife's family going back five generations. Our little Ivanka is the sixth of that name." But that doesn't last. Where names are concerned, poetry takes a backseat to practicality.

As soon as a kid acquires locomotion, she's gone. She doesn't need to be able to walk on two legs. Heck, she doesn't even need to be able to crawl. As soon as your kid figures out that flailing arms and legs aren't merely for expressing displeasure but can be harnessed for migration, she's out of there. Nature has given young children the triple advantage of being quick, quiet, and small enough to fit into tiny spaces. When you want to sleep, they're louder than a frat house on homecoming night. But when they're getting into things they shouldn't, they're like incontinent ninjas. Sometimes the only way you can find them is by following the smell.

So, with locomotion comes the need to summon the little tykes. And this is where practicality comes in. When you finally put that name to work, you'll regret not having picked an industrial-strength name like Bob. You can keep saying "Bob" until the cows come home. "Bob, where are you?" "Bob, come here!" "Bob, don't bite the cat!" But if you picked a poetic name, now is when you'll regret it. Try repeating "Beatrix" or "Jacinda" ad infinitum. This is why God invented nicknames. The nickname is the name you should have given your kid but were too embarrassed to pick. It takes a while to whittle a flowery name down to something that can be used easily on a day-to-day basis. And you can tell how much trouble a kid gets into by how quickly the parents adopt an industrial-strength nickname. Over the course of about three days, our lovely Ivanka became "Vonky," then "Schpanky," then "Schpank," then "Spank," then "Hank." Hank is an industrial-strength name. You can shout it all the livelong day, and the last use will be as potent as the first. It's one of those names that lends itself to yelling. You can put some serious air pressure behind that opening consonant, and the hard "k" at the end cuts off the sound to an immediate and ominous silence. "Hank" is the air horn of the naming world. "Beatrix" is the kazoo.

But nicknames bring their own baggage. At even at one syllable apiece, with a lot of children, nicknames can quickly add up to a lot of words to remember. Our last two kids, Alexander and Benjamin, were born just a year apart. Since we both abhor the nickname Alex, we announced his nickname before we left the hospital. "He shall be known as Xander." We also abhor "Ben," but since "Jamin" sounded like a reggae stoner, #6 stayed straight-up "Benjamin."

As they tend to be inseparable, my wife has taken to calling Xander and Benjamin (as a conglomerate), "Xanjamin." Kind of like Branjelina meets the Brady Bunch. "Xanjamin" exhibits a bit of creative flair, but at three syllables it's not industrial-strength. Plus, if you want to summon just one of them, you have to go back to either "Xander" or "Benjamin," which means that you now have three names to deal with instead of merely two. The efficient solution we evolved is to give each of them the same nickname: kid. Alexander is "kid." And so is Benjamin. If we need to refer to one of them, we say, "the kid." As in, "Tell the kid to take out the trash." And if the wrong one shows up, the other one is, by definition, "the other kid." As in, "Kid, come here. No, the other kid."

Last in the telling, though not the lineup, is Simon. Simon is the middle child. You hear about middle-child syndrome, where the poor middle child is ignored because he's not needy like the teenagers or cute like the babies. Middle children, the story goes, grow up to be meek and unsure of themselves. Middle children stay in the shadows of their more-outgoing siblings. Simon does not have middle-child syndrome. If there is an opposite of middle-child syndrome, that's what Simon has. Picture George S. Patton as a teenager. On a battlefield. In a tank. That's Simon. When told that their older brother would be staying at college over the summer, the other children were sad. Simon's response was: "Excellent. That means we all move up in rank."

Simon brings our total to six and, since six is divisible by two and three, we have developed a shorthand way of describing subsets of the children. The elder two are "The Majors." The middle two are "The Minors." And the kids are "The Minis." In order, they are girl-boy-boy-girl-boy-boy. That makes it natural to refer to the first three as "Round One" and the second three as "Round Two." With six kids, one can construct 63 unique subsets. Given that it would be quicker to identify them individually than to remember all 63 possible combinations, any further subsets aren't worth more than a "Am I looking at you? I mean you!" The entire set is known as "The Babies," a cute and cuddly name that, to their unending chagrin, we regularly use even though two are in college and one in graduate school.

What do you learn from having many children?

If you don't have a lot of children, you miss out on understanding subtleties of human nature. Humans are, hands down, the single most fascinating set of creatures on the planet. If you want to understand how humans work, just make a few, sit back, and watch them do their thing. But one or two won't do.

Humans are complex enough that each comes with serious individual quirks. To better understand humans in general you need to observe enough of them so the individual quirks average out and you get to see the commonality in their behaviors. How many are enough? Probably several hundred thousand. As that was outside our budget, we settled for six.

What sorts of insights have we gained into Homo sapiens?

> 1. *Children believe they are inventing the world as they experience it.* The child who, standing in front of you with chocolate all over his hands and face, insists that he most certainly did not eat the cake you left on the counter, believes he has invented lying. The kid thinks to himself, "A superb invention this: report a set of events that deviates from the set that actually occurred. Since no one was around to witness said events, the parents can only rely on my report." Had it occurred to the child that lying was invented about 20 minutes after language itself, he'd suspect that the parent would not only (a) know that lying was possible, but (b) be better at it than the kid, and (c) be able to spot it a mile away.
>
> This belief that just because they haven't experienced something before no one else has either continues on into the teenage years and can even be seen persisting into the adult years. Our teenager who thinks she's getting away with sneaking out of the house or making out with the neighbor kid doesn't consider that her parents are not merely parents. They are also past-teenagers who were interested in and did the same things she is doing. No, she's not getting away with anything. We're allowing her to believe she's getting away with something so she doesn't up her stealth game and actually succeed in getting away with something.
>
> When the British broke the Germans' secret code in World War II, they let Germany get away with sneak attacks so Germany wouldn't catch on to the fact that their code was broken. As soon as the Germans knew their code was broken, they'd change the code and the British would lose the ability to monitor them. The trick to clandestine observation is not to reveal that you're observing until it's absolutely necessary. So, to all you teenagers who think you're pulling one over on your parents: The good news is that you haven't screwed up enough for them to tip their hand. The bad news is that they know exactly what you've been doing.

2. *Children believe they are smarter than their parents.* The growing ubiquity of technological devices augments this belief. When I was a kid I was embarrassed that my father couldn't manage to program the simplest electronic device. And I don't mean "program" in the sense of writing a sequence of codes that instructs the device to perform certain functions. I mean "program" in the sense of any interaction more complicated than "turn it on." Here he was, a senior executive at a multinational corporation, and I, his ninth-grade son, had to set the time on his digital clock-radio because he couldn't figure out how to do it. If this, I thought, were typical of the caliber of mind populating corporate America, I would be running the country by my 18th birthday.

Now that I have my own ninth-grade son, on whom I rely to navigate Netflix, I realize the stark truth. It's not that I was a ninth-grade mental giant. It was that my father had so many other more important things to occupy his mind – things I had no idea even existed, like retirement portfolio contributions, mortgage escrow accounts, and tire rotation – that he didn't have the time or the inclination to occupy his thoughts with something he could much more easily accomplish by telling his son, "Go fix that flashing thing in my room."

Children believe they are smarter than their parents because children command nearly 100 percent of the knowledge they perceive to exist. History? Vikings, Columbus, America, World War II, moon landing. Done. Mathematics? Addition, multiplication, shapes, angles. Done. Science? Neil deGrasse Tyson, that guy in the wheelchair. Done. Philosophy? Socrates. Done. Children are very aware of the things they know. The irony, of course, is that they are so aware of the things they know because the number of things they know is embarrassingly small. The set of things that could possibly be known and of which they are completely unaware dwarfs the set of things they are aware of knowing, leaving them completely oblivious of their own rampant ignorance.

3. *Children have a keen but myopic sense of justice.* When you confront a child with the accusation that he has wronged someone, the child becomes a firehose of excuses as to why he is not, in fact, in

the wrong. The young child will rely on his weak lying skills. But the teenager – who has by this time in his life learned that he isn't good at overt lying and so has turned to lying by omission – will tell you things that are true but ancillary ("The Kid has done far worse things than this and you've never yelled at him for it.") or things that are true but not the whole truth ("She was being selfish because she wouldn't let me use her paints." Omission: I took them from her without asking and she demanded them back.). It is as if the laws of random chance apply differently to this child than to any other person on the planet: "You happened to walk in as I took a single swing at her, but you missed all the punches she landed on me." "I was going exactly the speed limit. I stayed four car lengths behind the guy, and had my eyes on the road the whole time. He must have slammed on his brakes really hard to stop so quickly that he forced me to run into him." Even though you caught the child red-handed, there are a plethora of airtight excuses why, in fact, this child is not in the wrong.

But allow the child to be the one wronged rather than the one committing the wronging, and all of a sudden the young defense attorney becomes the world's shrewdest prosecutor. The arguments, so reliable in his defense, that are packed with misunderstandings, questions of interpretation, and mitigating circumstances disappear. In their place are ice-cold facts and impeccable logic. In a way this is heartening. It suggests that the child has no problem comprehending justice. It's the equality of application that's lacking.

How hard is it to raise many children?

How hard is it to raise these delightful creatures? Raising small children is pretty easy, largely because they tend to cooperate in the venture. Sure, they don't want to go to bed or to clean up their rooms, but their desire to please you tends to win out. We observe that younger children who throw tantrums tend to come from overly permissive parents. Tantrum throwers, subconsciously, know that they are inadequate to running their own lives and so feel alone and unanchored when they are given too much free rein. As much as they say they want freedom, the reality of it terrifies them.

A much larger problem is raising teenagers. Teenagers don't want to be raised. Largely because (a) they believe they are already adults, and (b) they believe you don't know this and that's why you keep treating them like children. The code word for this in our house is "angst." Teenage angst is the eye-rolling, hair-flipping, dramatic-exiting, door-slamming that underlines the fact that parents either don't get it or, worse, actually take joy in making the teenager's life miserable.

Like most, our teenagers insist that we simply don't understand what it's like to be a teenager. (The fact that we've been where they are but they haven't been where we are doesn't appear to be noteworthy to them.) We assure them that we do understand. We've been teenagers, felt the conflicting emotions teenagers feel, experienced the heartbreak of finding then losing (repeatedly) the loves of our lives. (With 7 billion people on the planet, the probability of winning the Powerball jackpot is about 40 times the probability of meeting a "one true love." But you probably don't want to point that out to an angsty teenager.)

We absolutely do understand. And we tell our teenagers this. It's not that we don't understand what they're going through. It's that we don't care. Sure, the emotions surrounding their failures are strong. And they do deserve and have our support in dealing with their emotions. But the failures themselves are small potatoes and deserve to be treated as such. The teenager who is raised to believe that minor setbacks, disappointments, and embarrassments amount to extreme duress is a teenager who is not prepared to handle actual real-world problems-- like being fired or caring for a dying parent.

How do you handle money with so many children?

Raising lots of children is expensive, both in time and money, but not as much as you might believe. The joke about it being cheaper to buy a season pass than individual tickets is true. One child takes up all your time. Two children also take up all your time. Fortunately, there are only 24 hours in the day, so you're not any worse off. In a lot of ways more children are actually less work. Children tend to occupy each other. So while one child will badger you when he's bored or needs attention, two children can satisfy some of that need for each other. By the time you get to six or more children, you have enough for them to form teams. If anything, their ability to keep themselves occupied will cause them to have less need for interactions beyond their siblings. They'll also tend to raise each other. The key here is to get the first one right. Kind of like forming a template; character strengths and behavioral flaws in the first child tend to get replicated in the others.

When they get old enough to drive, they can drive each other places and even run errands for you, like grocery shopping. Which brings us to the monetary expense. Initially, the biggest expense is birthing and diapering them. Friends and family often pitch in for baby paraphernalia like playpens, car seats, and toys. When you have a kid, you are automatically plugged into a sort of underground hand-me-down economy. People with older kids are looking to get rid of clothes that no longer fit by handing them off to people with younger kids. It's a quid pro quo. The older parents avoid the guilt of throwing out reasonably good clothes, and the younger parents avoid the guilt of spending money on something the kid will outgrow long before it's worn out. If you have a lot of kids, you end up on both ends of the transaction. More than once, we've had friends hand down clothes to our younger kids that looked hauntingly familiar. Sure enough, they were clothes that our older kids had outgrown years before and that we had handed down to some other family. Like salmon returning home to spawn, the clothes had made their way back home, albeit with a few holes and permanent stains to record their journeys.

By far the largest expense is food. And this kicks in, as you might imagine, as they become teenagers. Most families will buy a gallon of milk, a dozen eggs, and a loaf of bread every week. Large families with teenagers will do this daily. Sometimes twice a day. Feeding two teenage boys simultaneously is a budget buster. Feeding four requires a home equity loan. It's actually a bonus when it comes to paying for college. A significant chunk of tuition expense is offset by the fact that someone else is feeding the hairy food vacuums.

The reality is that children are expensive and having more of them means having less of other things. When you have a lot of children, vacations are few and usually involve staying with extended family. Where other families might not think twice about going out to a restaurant, when you have a large family, a single venture like that can rival a car payment.

Oddly, one of the things we've learned is that money problems are most often not due to inadequate income but to profligate spending. People have a tendency to regard most things as necessities: My kid *has* to have a smartphone. My kid *must* participate in several sports. My kid *needs* a computer. Having lots of kids puts these things in perspective. Sure, your kid's friends text -- a lot. And if your kid doesn't also have a smartphone, he'll be left out of the texting circle. But just because kids spend a lot of time doing something doesn't mean that the thing is worth doing. (Either that or sitting slack-jawed in front of the television comes with serious benefits we've overlooked.) Ever look at a kid's texting history? Worrying about them being left out of their friends' texting circle is akin to worrying about them being left out of a mosh pit. Imagine Tolstoy typing *War and Peace* ... while drunk ... with his nose. That's the quality and quantity of communication they're missing out on. Teen texting is to meaningful communication what a flock of hungry pigeons is to *Swan Lake*. Yes, they'd *like* a smartphone. No, they don't *need* one.

When you have a lot of children, you realize that having more money doesn't make your money problems go away. You simply spend more and end up back in the same financial crunch you were in before -- only there are more zeros. This explains why politicians haven't managed to balance the federal budget since Eisenhower was president. (No, Clinton did not generate budget surpluses. The total federal debt rose every year he was in office.) Raising taxes just makes it easier for politicians to spend more money. It turns out that government is just like a household with a lot of kids. Only about 60 million times bigger. Don't get me wrong, bringing in income is critical when you're feeding a platoon of humans. But saving an extra dollar is actually more valuable than earning an extra dollar. When our household earns an extra dollar of income, because of taxes we are only 75 cents better off. But when we save an extra dollar, we are a full dollar better off. That means we should be spending about one-third more of our energy finding ways to save money than on finding ways to earn more.

Having a lot of kids means being more concerned with finances. But it also means making the kids more concerned with finances. And that's a good thing. We have friends who don't discuss their household's finances with their children because they want to shelter them from financial constraints. All that does is to produce children who believe that financial constraints don't exist. They then grow up to impose their bizarre belief on the rest of us by voting Democrat.

As an economist with six children, for me, teaching kids about money early on is a top parenting priority. In our house a first-grader gets an allowance and a "bank sheet" that is posted in the kitchen. Every time the child spends or receives money, he enters the transaction on the bank sheet. At the end of each month I check the calculations and post new bank sheets. Here are lessons you can teach with an activity like this:

> 1. *Money is the reward for work.* Emphasize that an allowance is not a right, but the reward for chores. If the chores aren't done, the allowance isn't paid. Note to the teenagers: No, you cannot give up

your allowance in exchange for being excused from chores.

2. *Money is real, whether it is cash or an entry on a ledger.* Children who don't learn this lesson grow up to become adults who think that a credit card isn't real money.

3. *You must monitor your finances.* If a child overdraws his account or fails to enter a transaction, charge a fine. There will be tears, and you will feel horrible, but don't give in. Note to the teenagers: Think this is unfair? Try overdrawing at a real bank.

4. *Living within an income means sometimes making painful choices.* Children who do not learn this grow up to become spendthrift adults because they never learned that getting something always means giving up something else. While shopping, if a child asks for something for herself, tell her to use her allowance. This seems harsh, but it is a valuable teaching moment and empowering. You will see the wheels turning in the child's head as she weighs the desire for the object against the necessity of paying. Note to the teenagers: Yes, I hear you saying that you can't live without this thing. But if you don't value the thing enough to part with your money, why should I part with mine?

5. *Making choices is empowering.* When you force the child to make a purchase decision, you run the risk of the child's making a poor choice. Advise your child, but allow her to make a poor choice if she insists. When the mistake becomes apparent, talk about what she could have done differently and what she'll do next time. It's painful to watch, but the child gains a growing sense of empowerment as she realizes that she is the one making the decision.

6. *Financial rights imply financial responsibilities.* Require the children to pay for birthday presents when they are invited to parties. You'll need to work with the younger ones; make sure they have plenty of time to save and remind them why they are saving. Painful but important: If they had the opportunity to save money for the present but didn't, don't let them go to the party. It sounds harsh, but it will only happen once. The powerful accompanying lesson: Responsibility means living with the consequences of one's decisions.

7. *Long-term saving is rewarding.* If a child saves his money for at least 12 months, I pay him 100 percent interest on the savings. Kids' time horizons tend to be too short for them to understand interest.

Paying a ridiculously high interest rate gets the kids' attentions. Each month, when I post new bank sheets, I show the interest they have earned so far on their savings. Even though they can't withdraw the money for 12 months, they can see the amount steadily growing.

A note on teenagers: There is nothing so endearing or aggravating as a teenager's myopic quest for "fairness." When she turned 16, my daughter informed me that it was unfair that she worked so hard for only a $20 allowance. "I want to be paid minimum wage for the work I do at home," she said. "Fine," I said. "Realy?" she asked. "Absolutely," I said. "Your labor is valuable, and it is unfair for me to take your labor without just compensation."

Astounded, she pressed me on the details. Would I pay her $7 for each hour that she worked? Yes. Would I pay her each week? Yes. Regardless of the number of hours worked? Yes. "Fine," she said, "That's fair." "No," I replied, "it isn't fair yet. You have a room in this house, use of the car, meals, clothes, electricity, water, insurance, and many other things of which you are likely unaware. If you believe that labor must be fairly compensated, then you must agree that your parents' labor—work that provides all these things—must be fairly compensated. To be fair, I must deduct your $7 per hour from the $800 per month that you will owe me for all these things that you currently get for free."

After the tears we had a talk about what it means to be a member of a family and to contribute to the household not out of pecuniary interest but out of love. For the first time she realized that my financial rules weren't there to restrict her freedom, but to help her learn how to exercise that freedom well.

Why not have a bunch of kids?

In the end children are expensive. They are messy. They are frustrating. They can be selfish and argumentative. They are also immense fun. They are creativity unencumbered by talent. They are slow to judge and quick to forgive. They love not out of reciprocity or personal gain but because that's what they do. They are joyful packets of energy that upend your life and wreck your plans in every way possible. They are the most wonderful creatures you will ever have the pleasure to know.

When you reach the end of your life, you will look back on career accomplishments that the world has long forgotten, and at hard-won money, power, and prestige that have long since faded into the mists of time. And you will know that the single greatest accomplishment any person can achieve in this life is to populate the world with children who love each other, care for those less fortunate, and walk humbly with their God.

Chapter Nine

Why haven't you flown first class?

Tim Chermak

Seriously.

The last time you booked a flight, did the possibility of investing in a first-class ticket even cross your mind? Was it an unrealistic, but *theoretically possible*, outcome?

Or, like most travelers, did you buy the cheapest ticket you could possibly find?

Be honest.

When you search for available flights, do you click to sort the results by lowest price? If you're like most travelers, the answer is yes. That much isn't surprising. We all want a good deal! It just *feels good* knowing you outsmarted the airlines and scored a bargain on tickets.

What I find incredibly interesting is that for most people, this decision is made *automatically*...without any conscious thought.

"What decision," you ask?

Exactly.

Choosing the lowest price isn't really a decision—it could be described as a "lack of" decision.

When most travelers order their airline tickets, it never even occurs to them that there is an upgrade option available. It never even occurs to them that they could purchase one of the coveted, oversized seats at the front of the plane. It never even occurs to them that being suffocated in a middle seat between two obese passengers suffering from weapons-grade halitosis is not...fate. It is not a predestined, unavoidable reality. In fact, quite the opposite. It's a choice.

Of course, price is one of many factors that goes into the purchasing calculation known as value. The *best deal* is not synonymous with "lowest price." Value is a more nuanced metric.

For example, a Ferrari is too expensive for *most drivers in most situations*. Spending hundreds of thousands of dollars on a car is not a realistic purchase. But how would the value calculation change if you were able to purchase a brand new Ferrari for just $50,000?

At that price the car is a bargain. It would be easy to flip it for a nice six-figure profit. Even if we didn't have access to the money, we would find a way to get 50 grand if it meant acquiring a brand-new Ferrari.

Interesting.

We would *find a way*. Instead of the usual default response, "I can't afford it," we would use our creativity to solve the problem. In doing so we would discover that we could afford it all along. All these years that we suffered through crying babies and restricted legroom we could have flown first class. We just chose not to.

In a free-market economy it's easy to take choice for granted. In the broader context of economic history, being free to choose is nothing short of a miracle. Not everyone has the luxury of going to a supermarket and seeing 10 different kinds of milk, eggs, and cheese. But many people can decide among 10 different grocery stores!

But we don't.

For most choices in life we decide early on what is and isn't realistic. And then we put that decision on autopilot, never to be considered again. How many times have you wanted to buy something but instead told yourself, "I can't afford it." This is a tragic mistake.

Our minds are so programmed to find the "best deal" that we implicitly forfeit the privilege of choice. For most people flying coach is a default decision, made without any conscious effort.

To be fair, our brains have a good reason for doing this. If we had to consciously evaluate the pros and cons of every decision, our brains would quickly become overloaded. Just like a computer with too many browsers open, our brains don't have enough processing power to *consciously* evaluate every choice.

And so most of our decisions are made subconsciously.

As soon as the brain recognizes a pattern, it tries to form a habit. Habits are the brain's way of streamlining the decisionmaking process. By eliminating the routine, everyday decisions, we can save our creative energy for more open-ended problem solving.

This is why we can perform some tasks automatically, almost without thinking. *Almost.*

Something as simple as walking up stairs is much more complex than we think. We don't consciously tell our left leg to rise, and then command our right leg to do the same. We don't send a conscious signal to our calf muscles to activate so we can climb the next stair. There are no neural messages sent to our arms to swing with just the right amount of momentum necessary to balance. All of that happens automatically below the threshold of conscious thought.

And the result is we are able to walk up and down stairs without thinking about it.

Unfortunately, we buy airline tickets the same way.

Last January I decided to test this theory. While most of my friends resolved to lose weight, quit smoking, or get out of debt, my New Year's resolution was categorically different. I decided to start flying first class.

My resolution was simple: I would fly first class on all flights. If I couldn't justify paying for a first-class seat, the trip probably wasn't an important enough use of my time.

Initially the resolution was about time management. It had nothing to do with upgrading my standard of living. I had been distracted by some business conferences that I probably shouldn't have attended, and I hoped that a commitment to buying expensive first-class tickets would kill this habit. I was using business trips as an excuse to avoid doing real work. It's always easier to network and take notes at a conference than it is to do the work of applying that knowledge in the real world. I was spending a lot of money on seminars, networking, and other business-related travel expenses. The money wasn't the problem (After all, it's tax deductible!). It was the time.

When I looked at the ratio of input to output (how many "awesome ideas"

I learned at events versus the ideas I actually implemented), I wasn't impressed. In fact I almost had a panic attack. I was spending a lot of time learning about new ideas, strategies, and trends. I was spending hardly any time actually implementing those ideas. Something had to change.

So I decided to impose an additional travel fee with my resolution. If I didn't think it was worth shelling out the extra cash for a first-class seat (usually double or even triple what a regular seat costs), I wouldn't go on the trip. This provided a useful litmus test for my addiction to conferences and other business trips. If it was worth $1,000-$2,000 on airfare, it probably *was* worth it. If not, I probably shouldn't go even for cheaper.

I was hoping my resolution would prevent me from flying, but a funny thing happened: I got addicted to flying first class. After indulging in the first-class experience, flying coach felt like cruel and unusual punishment.

What started out as a personal time-management experiment quickly evolved into a question I now ask myself almost every day: why not fly first class?

Of course I don't mean it literally. Outside the context of booking flights, asking myself this question is a simple reminder that cutting expenses is the coward's way of dealing with financial problems.

Instead of cutting expenses, address the real issue: lack of income.

For most of us this has never been a question. When we need to free up some cash, we look for things to cut. It never even occurs to us that half of accounting is about income—not expenses.

Expenses are paid for with income! When it comes to improving the financial condition of a company, both expenses and income are independent variables. They can both be tweaked. You can improve the financial health of an organization by growing revenues, slashing expenses, or a mixture of both.

If anything, expenses are a dependent variable, because how much you spend is usually determined by how much you *can* spend.

Personal finance is no different than corporate finance.

When it comes to our personal lives, most of us are convinced that income is a dependent variable. For some reason we believe that it's a fixed number that cannot be changed. And so we spend all of our energy trying to manipulate the only variable we *think* we have control over: expenses.

Instead of brainstorming new ways to create value, we ruthlessly analyze our expenses, trying to save a couple dollars here and there. Not only is this inefficient; it's also incredibly demoralizing!

Whenever I want to buy something I can't afford, I remind myself that that's bullshit. I *can* afford it. I'm just choosing not to.

In this way a circumstance becomes a challenge becomes an opportunity: an opportunity to think my way through a problem instead of raising the white flag of mental surrender.

"I can't afford it" is a crude, animalistic response. When you convince yourself that you can't afford it, you are sacrificing your highly developed frontal lobe (the brain's creativity factory) for what Seth Godin calls the "lizard brain" (the amygdala).

And it's a foolish trade.

The frontal lobe allows us to overcome obstacles using mind over muscle. There's a reason that humans rule the world, even though we are physically inferior to many other species: our minds are our competitive advantage.

When we need to cross a river, we don't worry about swimming. We build a bridge. When we need to warm up during a cold winter, we don't worry about gathering firewood. We turn up the temperature in our climate-controlled homes. For millennia we have worked smarter not harder. That is why we thrive when other species merely survive.

When we refuse to use our minds to solve problems, and instead pretend that the solution is out of our reach, we abandon the incredible gift that makes us uniquely human: our creativity.

When I started flying first class I discovered that upgrading your standard of living requires creativity.

That's it. Nothing more, nothing less.

The opposite is not true. Cutting expenses requires no creativity.

When faced with a purchasing decision that *feels* too expensive, most people's default response is "I can't afford it." They immediately retreat into a predetermined, fixed mindset of what they can and can't afford.

"I can't afford it" is really just a euphemism for *I'm not the type of person that flies first class.*

It's not a cash-flow problem. It's an identity crisis.

Much research has been done on how our self-concept determines our behavior (most notably by Stanford's Carol Dweck). If you think you can't afford to fly first class, your mind will agree with you.

However, when you challenge your assumptions, something interesting happens. Instead of preserving the status quo, your mind creates a new one from scratch.

Your subconscious mind is a yes-man. It goes along with whatever commands you give it. If you truly believe that you can afford to fly first class, your brain will immediately start creating possibilities to make it happen.

(For a more detailed and scientific explanation, Google *reticular activating system*.)

Creativity assumes that something new is being built. Cutting expenses requires no creativity. When your default response to a financial challenge is to cut expenses, you are not creating anything. You are *eliminating*. It's the opposite of creativity.

The short-term implications are damaging, but the long-term consequences are even worse.

Over time abdicating your creativity cultivates a scarcity mindset. The human mind is incredibly efficient at pattern recognition. As noted, if you repeatedly tell yourself that you "can't afford it," your brain will believe you. Eventually, you won't have to tell yourself anymore. It will become part of your identity.

Notice that all of the typical New Year's resolutions are about stopping something bad. They are about eliminating behaviors we aren't proud of. Instead of blazing new trails of progress, we fight to retake ground we have lost.

Most of us will fight 10 times harder to return to a sense of normalcy than we will to upgrade what we define as normal. If a salesperson used to earning $5,000/month hits a slump and is only producing $4,000/month, he will do whatever it takes to get back to normal. His self-concept depends on it: he is a $5,000/month earner! But ask him to replicate that same degree of change (a $1,000/month improvement) by going from $5,000/month to $6,000/month, and he will freeze.

It's not as easy as "working harder." You must first upgrade your expectations.

After years of conditioning, most of us are wired to preserve the status quo. We will always exert more energy on maintenance than improvement.

We gained the "freshman 15" in college (and maybe an additional 15 by senior year), and we want to *lose it*. So we resolve to hit the gym, and start ordering salads when we go to Chipotle.

Or maybe we have a little bit of credit-card debt. After reading the latest Dave Ramsey book we resolve to live debt free! As terrific as it sounds, this is a one-time event. Paying off a debt is certainly a good thing, but it creates no lasting change.

Compare this with a goal of increasing your income by 20 percent. If you did that, you could certainly pay off your debts. But once the debt was paid off you would continue to enjoy a higher standard of living.

Why don't we do this?

The real reason is surprisingly simple: it takes considerably more mental energy to *create* than to eliminate. Creating a new reality requires mental labor. It's easier to think of things we can go without (satellite TV, pricey Starbucks drinks, expensive refreshments at movies) than to think of new ways to add value to the world.

It's simple. Not easy, but simple.

To upgrade your income, increase the value you are adding to those around you. Whether you're an entrepreneur or an employee, this is a consistent economic reality: your income is a direct function of the value you create for other people.

Instead of using mental energy to cut expenses, use that same amount of energy to think of ways to add more value to the world.

When you do, *your* world will never be the same.

Solving perceived financial problems requires mental energy either way. Whether you are committed to flying first class or you're committed to paying down your student loans, it will require some mental firepower.

Why not choose to invest that energy in *creating* instead of eliminating? Most of us firmly believe that the only way to improve our well-being is through subtraction. We assume that a better life is only attainable by cutting out the bad stuff.

I'm not saying that building muscle is always preferable to losing fat, or that getting a raise is always better than saving up money to pay down debt. Obviously, every situation is different. But what if you could have your cake and eat it, too? When faced with a *this or that* decision, what if you could choose "yes" and get both? In other words, what if you could all but eliminate the opportunity cost of your choices?
It's possible. And trust me, when you see how simple it is, life gets much more interesting.

This is the technique I used a couple years ago to buy a brand new Cadillac with just $12,000.
I was 22 years old. At the time 12 grand represented my entire life savings. I needed to buy a car with that money. (The vehicle my parents had bought me at age 16 needed more repairs than it was worth.) I knew it would be foolish to spend all my money on a depreciating asset like a car, but I also didn't want to buy a junker that would require future repair bills. I needed to compromise with a car good enough to avoid expensive visits to the mechanic, but cheap enough to fit within my budget.

Decisions, decisions …

Chapter Nine

To make the situation even more complex, I wanted to put at least *some* of that capital into an interest-earning investment account. I wasn't a financial expert, but I was smart enough to know that it wasn't wise to store my money in a zero-interest checking account.

I had $12,000, and I expected this relatively small amount of money to purchase a reliable car *and* provide a foundation for my future retirement.

Oh, and one more thing. I had this crazy, unrealistic goal of owning a luxury car before age 25. Yeah, I know—a stupid idea, but it was always in the back of my mind.

I reasoned that *anyone* could save up enough money to splurge on a sweet ride when he's 50. But at that point, who cares? There are plenty of middle-aged men buying red sports cars already. Midlife crises are a fantastic opportunity for car dealerships!

That doesn't impress anyone.

But it would take extraordinary success (and perhaps ingenuity) to have enough money to drive a luxury car at a young age. It was a status symbol. It was proof of success. If you could afford a luxury car before age 25, well, *that* was interesting.

Or so I thought.

I categorized a luxury car as a BMW, Mercedes, Audi, Cadillac—any brand that people *aspired* to drive. A car that impressed people. As vain as it sounds, that was my goal. I wanted people to notice me!

Growing up, my dad always drove brand new Cadillacs. He would trade them in after a year or two and buy the newest model. As a kid I didn't think anything of it. I just liked the new-car smell when he would bring home the latest model.

Of course, ignorance can be bliss. When I transitioned from adolescence to adulthood, I realized that it's damn difficult to buy a luxury vehicle. It's hard enough to pay for rent, utilities, and all the other costs of being an adult. Most people don't have the margin every month to factor in a car payment that equals their mortgage! And they certainly don't have the money lying around to pay cash for such a vehicle.

But I was determined. For me it was a rite of passage. I wanted to be as successful as my dad, who grew up dirt poor yet became a cash-in-the-bank millionaire.

Looking back, my motives were silly. I'm guessing a psychologist would say it was about a desire to impress my father. And the psychologist would probably be right.

But it was more than that—it was about wanting something so badly you found a way to get it.
I definitely annoyed plenty of car salespeople. No one takes a college-age kid seriously when he walks into a Cadillac dealership. When you ask to test-drive a luxury car at age 22, the salesmen are skeptical, to put it nicely.

After a couple awkward test-drives with salesmen twice my age, I settled on a Cadillac ATS. That was the car I wanted to be seen in. I was going to do whatever it took to make it happen.

Common sense be damned.

I had $12,000 to spend, and no idea how to spend it. I could use that as a down payment and finance the rest of the price (a remaining balance of around 40 grand). But that would make it impossible to save for retirement. I needed to allocate at least *some* of that money towards an investment account.

I had read enough books (and sat through enough presentations) to know that the most important factor in saving for retirement is starting early. Compound interest can work magic with enough time. So if I spent all my money on a car, I would be sabotaging my future.

When I used the infamous "Rule of 72"[15] to predict how soon my $12,000 would compound into a million bucks, I realized that the opportunity cost of spending that money on a car was enormous.
It was financial suicide.

Beyond the opportunity cost, there was another cost I would need to overcome: the monthly payments on a $40,000 auto loan. The monthly payment would all but bankrupt me. Nice.

Fortunately, what I lacked in financial capital I made up for in creativity.

I decided to invest the $12,000 as a down payment on a rental property (a local triplex). When I subtracted the monthly expenses from the monthly rental income, I had almost $1,000 leftover every month. Not every year ... *every month*. At the time this was the equivalent of giving myself a 50 percent raise.

The best part? I didn't have to compromise between investing in my future and driving my dream car. I chose to do both at the same time.

The monthly profits from my real-estate investment provided enough money for me to purchase a brand new Cadillac (with red leather seats)! If I had used the money to buy a car, my capital would have depreciated in value every year. Eventually my $12,000 would be worth zero. Cars don't go up in value. They go down!

On the flip side, if I had put everything into mutual funds (or other traditional investments), I would have had little to nothing leftover for a vehicle. And it would have been impossible to achieve my goal of driving a luxury car before age 25.

My creativity bridged the gap between my finances and my goals.

Most people are content waiting years and years saving up money, hoping to one day have enough cash to purchase their dream car (or take a dream vacation, buy their dream house, etc.). They are subconsciously embracing a zero-sum approach to life. Instead of growing the pie, they spend their time trying to figure out novel ways of cutting it into smaller pieces. This is both frustrating and unfulfilling.

Society tells us that patience is a virtue. I suppose I agree. But creativity is even better.

By using my creativity I was able to avoid using subtraction (cutting expenses) to achieve my goals. Instead, I used *multiplication*, turning my $12,000 down payment into an investment yielding an annual return of almost 100%. This allowed me to simultaneously achieve my investment goals *and* my personal goals.

The house paid for the brand new car. And when the car loan is paid off, I will still have the house! It almost goes without saying that when the mortgage is paid off, the investment's return will accelerate accordingly.

Not a bad investment for a 22-year-old kid.

I had, and have, no special knowledge. I wasn't formally trained in finance, economics, or investing. I just used my creativity to see what others couldn't see.

When faced with a decision of *this or that*, I decided I would have both. Once the decision was made, my brain went to work to create a workable solution.

Jim Rohn once said that the most important part about setting goals is how they entice you to become the person it takes to achieve them.

I couldn't agree more.

There was nothing life-changing about flying first class until I realized there was something life-changing about *who I had become*. Sitting at the front of the plane will not solve your problems, but believing you are worthy of sitting at the front of the plane just might.

Just as when I used my creativity to buy a brand new Cadillac with $12,000, my commitment to flying first class forced me to *become the type of person who flies first class*. What was once my aspiration became my identity.

And that has made all the difference.

Chapter Ten

Why haven't you climbed a mountain?

Bob Ewing

Chapter Ten

"For how great the pleasure, how great, think you, are the joys of the spirit . . . in wondering at the mighty mass of mountains while gazing upon their immensity and, as it were, in lifting one's head among the clouds. In some way or other the mind is overturned by their dizzying heights and is caught up in contemplation of the Supreme Architect."
~ Naturalist Conrad Gessner (1516-1565)

"Ya see that mountain o'er dere? Yea, one of these days I'm gonna climb dat mountain!"
~ Mountain Music, Alabama (1982)

The air was cold in the afternoon on the 11th of April in 2009. My climbing partner Jeff and I were alone, deep in the Nevada desert. I was dangling upside down by a rope, staring at the ground spinning around more than a thousand feet beneath me. I had just taken a long screaming fall and couldn't figure out how get back on the rock and continue climbing. I tried—doing everything I possibly could—to no avail.

But I had to figure it out. It was our only way off the mountain.

A month earlier we were sitting at a DC airport together. It was early, the sun had yet to rise. Our plan was set: fly to Nevada and test ourselves with a long, difficult, rarely done climbing route called Resolution Arete, which summits Mount Wilson, the highest mountain in Red Rock Canyon. I had my heart set on it for years.

Bags packed full of climbing gear, we sat at the airport looking at each other, apprehensive and wondering if we'd get to board the plane. We were flying standby, a benefit of Jeff's wife. Turns out the flights were all booked. Before we could pretend to be upset, Jeff quickly pointed out, "I know we're both secretly relieved about this." We knew that summiting Mount Wilson would be an endurance test for us. But it would have to wait. We drove back to our homes that morning discussing how we would get to Nevada as soon as possible. A few short weeks later, we'd find out just how tough it is to climb Resolution Arete.

Initiation

I never would have started climbing if it weren't for the Supreme Court.

Why haven't you climbed a mountain?

Just before Christmas in the year 2000, while I was in the midst of college out in Ohio, unbeknownst to me a little-known law firm filed a little-known lawsuit in a little-known town in New England. But this law firm had some of the most brilliant legal minds working for it, and its lawsuit would ultimately unleash an explosion of outrage throughout the country, affecting the lives of countless people. Myself included.

The case centered on a simple question: may the government take your home and hand it over to someone richer if that richer person promises to generate more tax revenue with your property? The lawsuit worked its way through the legal system, all the way up to the highest court in the land. And in June 2005 the Supreme Court issued its controversial 5-4 ruling in favor of the government.

The infamous *Kelo* decision.

People went crazy. The law firm which brought the case, the Institute for Justice, burst into the national spotlight. Refusing to give up, IJ launched a multimillion dollar campaign, taking the fight to state courts, state legislatures, and the court of public opinion. IJ needed more resources, quick, so it hired several new people. One was an attorney named Jeff. Another was a media guy with, as Ant Davies puts it, an industrial-strength name: Bob.

(That's me.)

Outside of suing governments, Jeff's passion was climbing. Moving to a new city meant that he needed a new climbing partner. One of IJ's production guys, Isaac, had just started climbing. After hearing Jeff talk about his adventures, Isaac and I said that we'd like to join him. My brother Scott expressed interest as well. The four of us have been climbing together ever since, summiting vistas around the country and beyond.

Ten years after *Kelo*, nine state supreme courts, 44 state legislatures, and thousands of media stories have repudiated the high court's decision—and as a bonus I got to meet Jeff and Isaac. Without *Kelo* I likely never would have made a career in DC. And I almost assuredly would not have started climbing. I've always enjoyed outdoor activities, but I had never climbed before. To be honest, I never even thought about it. I didn't know it was an option.

I didn't know I could

Biologist Richard Dawkins opens his bestselling book *The God Delusion* with this:

> As a child, my wife hated her school and wished she could leave. Years later, when she was in her twenties, she disclosed this unhappy fact to her parents, and her mother was aghast: "*But darling, why didn't you come and tell us?*" Lalla's reply is my text for today, "*But I didn't know I could.*"

I didn't know I could.

How many things in life do you think this way about? Perhaps even more important, how many things in life *do you not even know* that you think this way about?

Until I started climbing, I didn't know I could.

I've never been the greatest athlete -- or the best student -- or the hardest working employee. But with climbing, none of that stuff matters. Everyone can enjoy climbing. Show up to any climbing gym on the planet, and you'll find a diverse array of people: young and old, short and tall, male and female, ripped and flabby, outgoing and shy, atheist and creationist, Democrat and Republican, Capulet and Montague. There will be climbs so easy your grandma can do them, and climbs so hard that no one but Spiderman could ascend them freely. But the motley crew of folks assembled will all be enjoying the gym together.

And notice that with most activities—from traditional sports to martial arts to games like chess—there is a winner and a loser. They are zero-sum. But climbing is different. Everyone, regardless of skill level, walks away having gained.

The bottom line is this: In climbing everybody wins. And just about every person who wants to climb can do it. Including you.

I have a quick action item for you to handle right now:

> Google *Eichorn Pinnacle*.

Do it. Google *Eichorn Pinnacle*. Check out the pictures. Find the one that resonates the most with you. Now take a moment to imagine yourself standing there, on the very top. Feel the rock beneath your feet. Feel the cool alpine breeze on your face. Feel the exhilaration deep inside you. Stare at the beautiful vistas that surround you. Watch the sun slip behind a distant mountain. Immerse yourself in the tranquility of the moment.

For years now, I've done exactly that. I've dreamed of standing on the summit of Eichorn Pinnacle.

Here's a cool truth: you can climb Eichorn Pinnacle.

Crazy as it looks, it's not a technically difficult climb. There's no reason you can't stand on that summit, if you want to do it. You don't have to be gifted athletically. You don't have to be brilliant or exceptionally hard-working. You don't need to be rich. You don't need a lifetime of experience. All you need is a desire to do it, a little climbing know-how, and a capable partner with experience (or a guide) to handle the logistics. It may look impossible, but you absolutely can do it!

And here's the kicker: if you learn enough about climbing, you can even be the one that leads your climbing team to the summit of Eichorn Pinnacle.

I'm typing this sentence on the 9th of August in 2015. In 18 days, on August 27, Jeff and I were to be on the summit of Eichorn Pinnacle. I would lead us to the top. I was finally going to do it. And it would be amazing.

Nevada

Jeff and I secured a standby flight to Las Vegas on April 10, 2009. We checked into a motel, bought food for our climb, packed up everything we'd need for Resolution Arete, and drove into Red Rock Canyon.

It's easy to get lost in the Canyon. Many climbers end up never finding the route they set out to climb. So we began with a scouting mission. We hiked through the desert for two hours, mostly uphill. We found the path we wanted. When it turned into a rock scramble, we continued up for awhile and stashed our packs under some boulders. Then we hiked out to the car. Back in town we had dinner and went to bed before the sun went down. We woke up at 3:30 a.m. on April 11 and set off for our adventure.

We reached our packs at sunrise and continued to scramble up the rock to the base of the climb. Resolution Arete begins with a scary traverse across a cliff to a crack. Few people do the climb, so there's loose rock and difficult route-finding. We ascended slower than anticipated.

The crux (or most challenging part) is a thin, overhanging finger crack about halfway up the 2,400-foot route. Imagine a small crack in the ceiling of the room you're in right now. An exaggeration for sure, but that's what it looked like to me from the hanging belay station below. It was this crux that would cause me so much grief.

Growth

Climbing is fundamentally about two things:

1. Personal growth
2. Connection

Italian climbing legend Walter Bonatti wrote that "climbing is not a battle with the elements, nor against the laws of gravity. It's a battle against oneself."

T.K. Coleman builds on Bonatti's insight in this very book when he writes that "the challenges you'll have to overcome, the fears you'll need to face, the mistakes you'll make, the ecstatic moments you'll experience, the people you'll meet—these will all be triggers activating aspects of your soul that you never knew existed."

These sentiments encapsulate my experience with Resolution Arete. As I hung from that rope high above the ground, I was terrified. I was physically and mentally exhausted. All I wanted to do was give up.

You know how sometimes you try really, really hard to do something, but you just can't do it? What happens next? You typically have a couple of options: you can give up, or you can give the task to someone else to do. But what if those options are taken away from you? What if your only option is to do it anyway? And what if your life—and your friend's life—depend on your figuring it out?

That's what I had to do on Resolution Arete. Jeff could yell advice to me, but ultimately, I had to make it happen. I had to calm my mind and focus completely on figuring out what to do. I had to find a way to get through the crux and keep climbing.

Since I was hanging away from the mountain, I knew that I had to ascend the rope. I needed to build a foot sling and connect it to the rope. But my hands were cold, and I was shaking; I couldn't do it right. I tried building the crude system, but it kept failing. I would move up the rope a couple feet and then slide back down.

Austrian mountaineer Heinrich Harrer, author of *Seven Years in Tibet*, wrote that "you cannot completely summon all your strength, all your will, all your energy, for the last desperate move, until you are convinced the last bridge is down behind you and there is nowhere to go but on." I knew there was nowhere to go but on. After some time I built the system and summoned the strength to climb up the rope. I placed my trembling right hand into a crack in the mountain and attempted to pull my body back onto the rock—and then I watched as my hand slowly slipped out. I fell back down again, dangling upside down in the open air.

Climbing forces you to accept reality. You must look objectively at your situation and deal with it. Each climb is like a puzzle, a challenge waiting for you to solve. To do it you must free your mind. You must overcome your fear of falling, your fear of failing, your fear of the unknown. You must ignore the past and the future, and focus your mind completely on the present moment—a moving meditation. You develop an understanding with yourself and the world around you, a peace in that moment. You are Zen. And in this process of being, you overcome. Your confidence, courage, and self-worth grow.

Jeff learned to climb in Japan. One of his mentors was a young Japanese guy, a local legend who climbed harder and better than anyone else. Jeff asked his mentor for advice on how to improve as a climber. This was before the days of climbing gyms, so Jeff figured he'd suggest some outdoor training regimen. But instead his mentor said this: *men-ta-ru toh-ray-neen-gu*. Mental training. Free your mind. Focus. Visualize the climb. He taught Jeff that you can build your climbing skill anywhere simply by disciplining your mind.

Climbing makes you mentally strong. Once you push yourself to your limit on the rock, problems you face back on the ground seem small. The rest of life's challenges become less daunting. The discipline that you cultivate applies to other aspects of your life: your career, your relationships, your desires. And when you have that battle against yourself, when you are forced to dig deep and do something that seems impossible—something you just can't do, yet have no other option but to do it—once you figure it out, you have an epiphany. Your mind expands. You grow.

Climbing makes you physically strong. Your entire body, muscles and ligaments from head to toe, get worked in a way that is impossible to do lifting weights in a gym. Perhaps more important, climbing inspires you to keep your body fit. I'll be visiting Yosemite twice a year for the next few years, and I have to be in shape for each trip. While the best way to train for climbing is to actually climb, you also want to have a general base level of fitness. Before each trip to Yosemite I will make sure that I meet three fitness benchmarks: 9 percent body fat, 5:45 mile, 325-pound deadlift. Without climbing, I would lack the motivation to stay fit.

Not every climb pushes you to your limit. You don't have to experience Resolution Arete to understand the essence of climbing. At its heart climbing is fun. It's going to the climbing gym and playing. It's going outside and playing. What better way is there for an adult to experience the magical, carefree joy from childhood than taking a few days off work and playing outside with friends? The British mountaineer George Mallory explained this well when he wrote, "What we get from this adventure is just sheer joy."

The most famous climbing book is called *The Freedom of the Hills*. Being in the mountains, unplugged from electronics and your typical daily stresses, makes you feel freedom and joy in a way that's hard to capture elsewhere. But there's a more important freedom that climbing provides. *The Atlantic* recently published a feature about an epidemic facing our country: college students graduating without a sense of autonomy—lacking self-worth, direction, and an ability to succeed in the world. Their "helicopter" parents hover over and baby them, depriving them of their freedom to fully develop. Climbing has the opposite effect; being empowered to overcome obstacles fosters self-discovery.

Climbing gives you the freedom to grow.

Connection

Climbing is about connection.

Sure you are physically connected to your partner through a rope, but that's not what I'm talking about. Have you ever truly placed your life in someone else's hands? Has anyone ever trusted his or her life completely to yours? Trusting your life to another, and having him trust his life to you, changes you. And it changes your relationship with your partners. It's the kind of connection that only comes when you face death. Life becomes poignant.

Have you ever stood on top of a narrow mountain peak—one accessible only by scaling its steep cliffs—alongside a handful of friends, staring together at the horizon stretching all around?

This experience is profound.

Imagine that you and I just scaled the sheer walls of Oregon's infamous Monkey Face. We are standing on the summit, just us and a few other climbing friends alone on top. In fact, take a quick glance now at my bio picture in the back of this book. Imagine being there with Scott, Jeff, Isaac and me. Imagine watching the sunset together, as we did, and then rappelling back to the ground in complete darkness. Think about how that entire experience would feel. Imagine the connection you and I would share during those moments—and after.

The other day I was talking with a good friend of mine, Price. He hit me up on gchat about a book he's reading, just a casual conversation, the way friends do. I tried to convince him to join us on our upcoming Yosemite adventure. I met Price in 2008 on a climbing trip in Red Rock Canyon. We got together again to scale the South Six Shooter (it looks just like it sounds) and the Castleton Tower in Utah. I just checked my climbing log: it's been six years since I've seen Price. And as I type this, I'm realizing that Price and I have only seen each other twice in our entire lives. That shocks me—I can't believe I've only done two trips with him, and I can't believe it's been six years since we've hung out—because he's a close friend. Once you share an experience like the Castleton Tower with someone, your connection stays deep. (I documented this climb. You can watch it by Googling *Bob Ewing Castleton Tower playlist*.)

Chapter Ten

I'll never forget that Utah adventure with Price. For several nights we sat around the same campfire, yet—like Heraclitus's river—each night we had a different gathering of people: from doctors and lawyers to vagabonds. Climbers from around the planet connected for a moment through our mutual desire to experience the freedom of the hills. We would share stories and contemplate—as Conrad Gessner did five centuries ago—how the rock draws you in, breaks you down, builds you back up, and fills you with joy.

The climbing culture is built upon a mentorship connection. And as Jeff has mentored me, I have mentored others.

I took my friend Pericles climbing in December 2012. It was his first multi-pitch adventure. We made it to the summit at sunset. As we worked our way to the rappel station to descend, we figured no other parties were on the mountain. The official season was over, so the climbing schools were closed and no one was around for help. If we got in trouble, we'd have to rescue ourselves. Halfway through my descent, I noticed the faint light from two headlamps penetrating the darkness below me. Two climbers were stuck and in trouble. The temperature was near freezing. One of the climbers was almost hysterical. They had a third member in their party up on the summit. But they were too far away to communicate. Pericles, who had not yet begun rappelling, was high enough up that he could shout to their friend. And we had two-way radios with us, so through Pericles and me the troubled team was back in contact. Working together we got all three climbers onto my ropes and down the mountain safely. Less than six months later Pericles returned to that same mountain as a knowledgeable climber and safely led a team to the summit and back down to the ground.

Right now my primary climbing partner is my friend Roger. We are members of a local gym, Earth Treks. Although we haven't known each other many years, our connection became deep enough that he asked me to be a groomsman in his wedding. His primary reason to train is so he can take his wife climbing outside, sharing memories together that will last a lifetime.

I actually was climbing when I got married, in the ultimate expression of connection. Jeff and Isaac served as groomsmen. Scott performed the ceremony on a narrow mountain peak. My other brother, John, took pictures that went viral online and ended up published in news outlets on every continent that has news outlets (Sadly, no Antarctica). My wife and I were featured in *London's Telegraph* as a photo of the week, on *Good Morning*

America, and on my personal favorite, Australia's top morning show *Sunrise*.

Climbing is sublime. Not only do you connect deeply with your partners, you build a mystical connection with the natural world. There's a French painting of a man all alone staring at a mountain sunset. The caption reads: "How beautiful this would be if only I could share it with someone." In climbing you have this experience all the time, except you always get to share it with someone. In fact it goes beyond this, as you enjoy breathtaking works of nature inaccessible to non-climbers. You see the world from a unique vantage point.

Psychologist Jon Haidt explains in his fantastic book *The Happiness Hypothesis* that happiness requires not just personal growth but also deep connections and relationships. As he puts it, happiness comes from between. We must build meaningful connections with other people, as well as with the world around us.

When I read Haidt's insights into how to lead a happy, meaningful life, I feel like he's describing climbing.

Risk

Of course, climbing is not for everybody. Some people are committed to staying indoors with their feet planted firmly on the ground. Others would rather not push themselves to their physical and mental limit. And many simply don't want to take the risk, which is inherent in the vertical world.

H.L. Mencken, the Sage of Baltimore, wrote: "They have an unsurpassed view of the scenery, but there is always the possibility that it may collide with them." He was describing hot air balloonists, but the description applies to climbers just the same.

Last year I was with Scott and Jeff on an alpine mountain called Matthes Crest when a guy climbed past us, alone and unroped. We exchanged brief salutations, and he was on his way. We'd find out later that his name was Brad Parker. He had just proposed to his girlfriend on a nearby mountain peak. She said yes. He called his father to share the good news and say that it was the happiest day of his life. Tragically, it was also his last. Shortly after passing us he slipped. Being unroped, he fell to his death.

If you decide to climb you must understand the risks you are undertaking. George Mallory, who I quoted above, died young while attempting to summit Mount Everest. His body wasn't discovered for 75 years. Every season from his disappearance to today, there have been climbing fatalities. All are tragic. But almost all are preventable. You can mitigate the vast majority of your risk by using common-sense safety measures, understanding and applying proper techniques, and knowing your limit.

Wisdom comes from experience. There are several things I have learned during my time on the rock, numerous ways I have created to avoid challenging situations, and wisdom I apply today.

Resolution

Eventually I got through the crux on Resolution Arete. Unfortunately, the next pitch wasn't much better. It is also technically difficult, and I was too blown out mentally and physically to climb it well. I struggled. We realized that it would be impossible to complete the entire route that day, so we'd have to find a place to sleep on the rock for the night.

We each brought a space blanket. You always have one in your pack when you climb outside, though you never plan to use it. We found a small ledge, connected ourselves to the wall, and did our best to lie down. The ledge isn't big enough to stretch out, so we curled up. When the sun went down, it got windy and cold. Very cold. Jeff's blanket tore apart as he moved around for warmth. We shivered and stared down at the lights of the Vegas strip in the distance—such a contrast in conditions! We spoke and laughed, thinking about how different the extravagant Dionysian exploits happening under those lights were compared to our situation. We did not sleep so much as endure the darkness until the sun rose.

We packed plenty of water for one day, but not enough for two. Several hundred feet of climbing into the second day we ran out of water. We were dehydrated. I sympathize with Peter Neiger's cracked lips on that brutally hot New Mexico day during his incredible biking adventure that he describes in these pages. Our lips cracked to the point that they bled. Thankfully, the upper portion of Resolution Arete had snow. We packed it into our water bottles and sipped it as it melted.

We made it to the summit. But as the cliché goes, when you get to the top you're only halfway there. Resolution Arete does not have a descent path. And the directions are vague at best. We bushwhacked and down climbed, unsure if we were going the right way. We came to a waterfall with a rappel rope. We backed it up with our gear and descended. Beneath the falls we built another rappel station with our own gear (leaving it behind) and descended further. As the sun set on the second day we made it to the wash. We raced across the boulders as fast as we could, our climbing gear clanging, Jeff holding up my cell phone desperate to get a signal. When it came he immediately called his wife. She was deeply relieved to hear his voice. She said the rescue helicopter was minutes from departure.

Inside the car, free at last from our harnesses and gear, completely exhausted, dehydrated, and bleeding from our cracked lips, Jeff turned to me and said, "Well I don't even know what to say about that." We drove to Las Vegas in silence.

There's an old mountaineer saying: "When you climb a mountain, you bring part of it back with you." Jeff and I will always carry Resolution Arete with us. It forged who we are today.

Climb on

It's been several years since that epic event. Time moves on. I've since left IJ to pursue a career at the excellent Mercatus Center at George Mason University. Jeff started a family and moved to Texas. Scott lives in Chicago. Isaac travels often. But, thanks to climbing, none of that holds us back. We still get together every season to unplug and play outside.

Climbing to the top of a mountain with a close friend, placing your lives in each other's hands, is an experience unlike any other. What better way is there to feed the wanderlust and commitment to adventure embedded in our being—that inescapable yearning to behold the world that Courtney Derr explains in this book? Italian poet Francesco Petrarca wrote that while standing on top of Mount Ventoux in France, "I was so affected by the unaccustomed spirit of the air, and by the free prospect, that I stood as one stupefied."

I can't predict the future, but I can say this: I will climb for the rest of my life. I will stand stupefied on mountaintops on every continent. I will share these experiences with some of my dearest family and friends. They will be among the most intimate and meaningful moments of my life.

There are countless mountain summits out there waiting for us. Beckoning. Luring. I've had the fortune to tick off a few celebrated ones already: Australia's Mount Arapiles, Carolina's Stone Mountain, Oregon's Monkey Face, Tuolumne's Matthes Crest, Utah's Castleton Tower, West Virginia's Seneca Rocks, Yosemite's Half Dome, Nevada's Mount Wilson.

Everyone has different goals in life. The same is true with climbing. Many climbers are content doing all their playing in a gym. Some are satisfied with nothing more than an occasional outing to a local park. And some of the best climbs in the world are not difficult. In two weeks Jeff and I will take our friend Renee up a scrambling romp called the Regular Route on Sunnyside Bench that tops out at the Lower Yosemite Falls swimming hole. You can do this wonderful climb—and when you get to the top you'll be rewarded with an incredible view while swimming right in the middle of one of the tallest waterfalls in North America: It's among the most magical and cathartic experiences imaginable.

That's the beauty. Climbing is what you choose to make it. Regardless of your level of commitment, if you choose to climb I promise you two things will happen: you will grow as an individual, strengthening your mind and body while discovering more about yourself; and you will build meaningful connections. Climbing is, paradoxically, an expression of both individuality and connection.

I all but assure you that your happiness and fulfillment will increase.

One example of the unique ego boost climbing gives you: Jeff and I summited Half Dome recently. There were more than a hundred tourists on top, having ascended via an arduous hike that culminates in the famous and scary metal cables. It's likely the hardest thing many of them had ever done. When those tourists, standing proud upon that fabled peak, see you appear covered in climbing gear, they stare at you, dumbfounded. They ask you about climbing. They ask to take a picture with you. We had a strikingly beautiful woman walk away from two tall shirtless rippling studs to get her picture taken and hang out with us.

That makes you feel like a superhero.

Why haven't you climbed a mountain?

You may find that just a little climbing will suffice. Or you may get full-on addicted. Yosemite climbing legend Chuck Pratt wrote, "I cannot imagine a sport other than climbing which offers such a complete and fulfilling expression of individuality. And I will not give it up nor even slow down, not for man, woman, nor wife, nor God."

The greatest climb in the world ascends the greatest rock formation in America. The place is Yosemite. The rock is El Capitan. The route is The Nose. Every climber's dream is to climb it, yet few do. It doesn't demand a perfectly sculpted body, or a brilliant mind, or Bobby Fischer's work ethic. It simply requires training and determination.

In 2018 I will climb The Nose. Jeff agreed to do it with me. We're on a four-year training plan. We'll climb the route in three days. At some point afterwards Scott and I will climb it together. And after that, perhaps I'll ascend The Nose with Isaac, Pericles, Roger, Price, and others in my life who are important to me and willing to make the trek. Perhaps I'll climb it with my grandkids. Perhaps I'll climb it with you. The memories will be unforgettable. The stories we create during these adventures, as Sylvia Culp once told T.K. Coleman, will last for the rest of our lives and, in a deeper sense, make us who we are.

A year after ascending The Nose, Jeff and I will return to Mount Wilson. We will bring with us an extra decade of experience and wisdom. On the 10th anniversary of our epic adventure—in 2019 the 11th of April falls on a Thursday—we will crush Resolution Arete and summit Mount Wilson in victory.

We will conquer the mountain that once almost conquered us.

I mean, why not?

Conclusion

Why haven't you started yet?

Isaac Morehouse

Conclusion

I thought about putting a book like this together for a few years. Then it occurred to me one day just how ironic it was that I hadn't acted on it, given the theme of the book. Even having a deep belief in the practice of flipping the burden of proof, I struggle to implement it. I had to face myself and admit that no good reason existed to hold back on getting this project done. Fear, embarrassment, ego, laziness, and other reasons existed, but they were all reasons I don't want defining my life. So I pulled the trigger.

There are a lot of big crazy things you could go after. When you start asking "why not?" instead of "why?" a lot of assumed reasons for not taking drastic action will melt away. This might cause a bit of a personal crisis. You'll run low on excuses for not living a life you love.

I think it's a lot harder to do what you love in life than to merely exist.

Once you begin asking "why not?" you'll find it's a long and difficult process to discover what you love, what truly makes you come alive. It includes a series of epiphanies about your own errors of judgement and direction. It demands brutal self-honesty. It requires tedious and dangerous trial and error. It cannot be found by mere reflection, but deep reflection has to occur alongside experimentation. None of this is easy, and you're never done. You change, and what makes you come alive changes. The journey toward it is endless, and adaptation and adjustments of your goals are continuous.

That's just to discover what you love. Once you've begun to remove the chaff and home in on a direction that fulfills you, actually moving in it is even harder. You have to muster the grit and determination to move toward it, even when the individual steps themselves are grueling. You have to continue to remind yourself of what really awakens your love of life and not let yourself off the hook for pursuing anything less.

It's much easier to find and do what you mildly enjoy, what you can tolerate, or even what you hate. Anyone can stop the discovery process short and find what feels comfortable in the short term. Anyone can choose not to chisel away the distractions, not to get to the core of what fulfills. Anyone can treat what he or she loves as an unattainable object that exists only to torment and tease. Anyone can come up with mediocre, safe, reasonable, sound, and predictable goals and activities.

People say that when you do what you love you never work a day. It's easy to hear that and envy those whose profession seems to be something they have a lot of fun with. It is true that when you're in the zone pursuing your passion, it doesn't feel like work. But discovering that zone and making yourself enter it is more work than anything.

Some people think work is hard because they're not doing what they love. In reality, they haven't been able to do what they love because they're not willing to work hard enough.[1][16]

Finding and re-finding what you love, and moving toward it every day, are the hardest things in the world. They are also the most worthwhile. The process begins with flipping the burden of proof on that break from the norm and instead demanding really damn good reasons to persist with the status quo.

The thing is, you can't really know whether a big change is going to be more fulfilling than whatever you're currently doing unless you try it. Asking "why not?" is a start, but when the reasons aren't clear, no amount of analysis or theorizing will do. You need field experiments. You need action.

In the first chapter Zak talked about taking the pressure off of yourself when it comes to living your best life by not seeking that elusive perfect plan, but rather by testing lots of things and simply building a list of the things that you hate. As long as you're not doing things that make you dead inside, your exploration is headed in the right direction.

There is nothing left but to try it. Did you learn to ride a bike by weighing the pros and cons or studying the lives of great bikers? Did you learn to walk or talk or swim by contemplating the risk and reward or reading inspirational texts?

You just tried.

When you ask "why not?" and you can't muster a solid list of reasons, it doesn't mean whatever you're considering is the silver bullet to your happiness. Courtney Derr described a pretty rough experience traveling the world and realized it wasn't everything she and her husband wanted. But now she knows. That knowledge could not have been had any other way, and living without an answer to the question "why not?" can bring a lot of regret.

Regret does not lead to happiness.

When you have no "why nots?" the thing to do is jump in. Try it. If you get a few metaphorical smacks in the face, now you've got your answer and one more thing to add to your "don't enjoy" list. You'll also come out the other side a better person than you went in. Guaranteed.

Make a list of ideas that have been tormenting you for a while. Ask "why not?" If no real, good reasons materialize, plot a plan to try them out, one at a time.

It's time to put down the book and go do something awesome.

Why not?

Why Haven't You Read This Book?

About the Authors

About the Authors

Ben and Nicole Angelo

Nicole Angelo is the sweetest person you'll ever meet. She owned and operated fashion and record store i heart ipanema in Kalamazoo until moving to LA. She's a vegetarian health nut who loves sunshine daydreaming with her husband.

Ben Angelo is head roaster for Stumptown Coffee Roasters in LA and serves as resident DJ for the SCAA Roasters Guild. He makes beats for his label Reckless Rogues and loves historical musicology. He met his dream girl Nicole 15 years ago and they've been kickin' it ever since.

Tim Chermak

Tim Chermak is a marketing consultant specializing in lead generation and conversion. He is author of the book *Main Street Marketing*. He co-founded FrontDesk (a company that makes marketing software for small businesses) and Platform (a digital marketing agency specializing in real estate). He lives in Naples, Florida, with his wife and their two dogs.

T.K. Coleman

T.K. Coleman is the co-founder and education director for Praxis, a 12-month apprenticeship program that combines a traditional liberal-arts education with practical skills training, one-on-one coaching, academic mentoring, group discussions, professional development workshops, and real-world business experience. T.K. is an avid lover of ideas and blogs regularly on personal development, education, and philosophy at *tkcoleman.com* and the Praxis blog at *discoverpraxis.com/blog*.

Antony Davies

Antony Davies is associate professor of economics at Duquesne University, Mercatus Affiliated Senior Scholar, and Strata Research Fellow. Davies has authored over 150 op-eds for, among others, the *Wall Street Journal, Los Angeles Times, Forbes, Investor's Business Daily*, and *New York Daily News*. His YouTube videos on economics and statistics have garnered over three million views. In addition to teaching at the undergraduate and Ph.D. levels, Dr. Davies was chief financial officer at Parabon Computation, president and co-founder of Paragon Software, and associate producer of *FI$H: How an Economy Grows*, at the Moving Pictures Institute. Dr. Davies earned his B.S. in economics from Saint Vincent College, and Ph.D. in economics from the State University of New York at Albany.

Courtney Derr

Courtney Derr is an advocate for freedom by day and a passionate traveler, wannabe gastronome, and writer by night and weekend.

She was born and raised in Las Vegas, NV, where she and her sisters could often be found hanging off a rock wall or playing in a creek. She attended the University of Washington in Seattle, earning a semi-useless degree in political science. A youthful dalliance in politics brought her to DC, where she lived for eight years before quitting her job for a year-long journey with her husband through Southeast Asia, the Middle East, and Europe.

Courtney lives for travel, food, gardening, and the great outdoors. She currently resides in Portland, OR, with her husband and dachshund Pappy Van Winkle, and works for the DC-based Institute for Humane Studies, a nonprofit dedicated to helping students and professors advance the principles and practice of freedom in their careers and lives. You can read more of her travel writing at *wanderrlust.com*.

Bob Ewing

Have you ever seen *the YouTube clip* of Justin Bieber riding a Segway? Check it out. The one from Glendale Arizona in 2010. That's what every day is like for Bob. People constantly tell him that he looks like Ryan Gosling, Channing Tatum, and Denzel Washington—except he's taller and more ripped than them.

Like Groucho, Bob was born at a very early age. The rumors of his childhood are true: when he was seven his mother sold him to the Gypsies. But to her credit, she used the money to buy Bob's brothers a Nintendo. He's never been in a Turkish prison. He's never had Quaaludes, but after seeing *The Wolf of Wall Street*, he's curious. He's never met Bob Monkhouse, but just like he did, Bob wants to die peacefully in his sleep—not screaming and terrified like his passengers.

According to Bob, Pink Floyd's *The Wall* is the greatest music ever made by mortals—this excludes Poison, of course, since they are Gods. Unskinny Bop just blows him away. Ewing insists that the four best short stories are *Biscuits* by Doug Adams, *Small Fry* by Anton Chekhov, *The Last Rung on the Ladder* by Stephen King, and *The Egg* by Andy Weir. They're all online. You should read them right now.

After finishing this book, of course.

Isaac Morehouse

Isaac Morehouse is an entrepreneur, thinker, communicator dedicated to the relentless pursuit of freedom, and an advocate of self-directed learning and living. He is the founder and CEO of *Praxis*, an intensive one-year program combining real-world business experience with personal coaching, professional development projects, and interdisciplinary education for those who want more than college.

Isaac has been involved in a number of business and nonprofit start-ups, and loves connecting people and helping them discover and realize their dreams. He writes, speaks, and teaches on entrepreneurship, economics, education, philosophy, freedom, communications skills, how to change the world, and an assortment of other topics. He has a weekly *podcast* and is the author of hundreds of articles and *Better Off Free* and *The Future of School*. He is coauthor of *Freedom Without Permission*.

When he's not with his wife and kids or traveling the country and building his company, he can be found smoking cigars, playing guitars, singing, reading, writing, getting angry watching sports teams from his home state of Michigan, or enjoying the beach.

Levi Morehouse

A passion for entrepreneurs paired with a love of technology and diverse experience in accounting, finance, and business strategy led to Levi founding Ceterus in 2008. Before Ceterus, Levi worked as a CPA in public and then private accounting. Levi graduated from Western Michigan University and currently lives in Mount Pleasant, South Carolina, with his wife, Alicia and their children.

About the Authors

Peter Neiger

Peter Neiger is originally from Gresham, Oregon, but left the Pacific Northwest after joining the Army in 2001. After four years of service and two combat deployments as an infantryman with the 82nd Airborne Division, he discovered a passion for adventure and travel. Thinking he needed a college degree to succeed, he moved to South Carolina, where he earned a BS in economics from the College of Charleston. He then moved to Washington, DC, where he spent three years working for education nonprofits before quitting and cycling across the country in the summer of 2012. In Los Angeles he worked for a high-end executive-protection and private-investigation firm for two years before beginning a multiyear bicycle ride around the US. He is currently traveling with his partner Anna and their two-year-old dog Higgins and works remotely as a writer/researcher for a community development consulting firm.

Jeffrey Tucker

Jeffrey Tucker is Director of Digital Development for the Foundation for Economic Education. He is also Chief Liberty Officer and founder of Liberty.me, the global liberty community with advanced social and publishing features, executive editor of Laissez Faire Books, research fellow at the Acton Institute, policy adviser of the Heartland Institute, founder of the CryptoCurrency Conference, member of the editorial board of the Molinari Review, an advisor to the blockchain application builder Factom, and author of five books. He has written 150 introductions to books and many thousands of articles appearing in the scholarly and popular press.

Zachary Slayback

Zachary Slayback is an entrepreneur and writer focusing on education, innovation, and philosophy. He is an Ivy League dropout and speaks and writes regularly on college, the negative effects of elite education, and how we can improve education for the individual and society at large. He believes that entrepreneurs are the primary actors of social change.

Zak is a founding team member of and business development director for *Praxis*. He has been published at *Newsweek*, the *New York Examiner*, the *Daily Caller*, the *Pittsburgh Post Gazette*, the *Christian Science Monitor*, the Foundation for Economic Education's *Anything Peaceful*, among others, and has also appeared on *The Glenn Beck Program* and *HuffPost Live*. He's spoken at Coin Congress SFO, The Thiel Foundation Summit, regional Students For Liberty conferences, and elsewhere.

Why Haven't You Read This Book?

Notes

Notes

[1] For more on the destructive nature of competition, see *Zero to One: Notes on Startups, Or How to Build The Future* by Peter Thiel and Blake Masters (Crown Business, 2014).

[2] Full disclosure: the friend was Isaac Morehouse and the startup was Praxis, with whom I still work.

[3] http://www.paulgraham.com/top.html

[4] For more on the idea of mimetic theory, visit *www.imitatio.org*

[5] *Zero to One*, 68-69.

[6] For more, see: http://zakslayback.com/2015/04/01/the-steve-jobs-fallacy-of-opting-out-of-college/

[7] For hacking failure, see: https://medium.com/on-breaking-the-mold/failure-is-overrated-hacking-failure-for-success-e7b0c08591f9

[8] See: http://www.usnews.com/education/blogs/the-college-solution/2011/03/01/the-ivy-league-earnings-myth

[9] Abraham Maslow was an American psychologist who developed a theory of health based on fulfilling specific needs. This "hierarchy of needs" theorized that in order for people to reach their potential (self-actualization) certain other needs must be met in a certain order: physiological needs (food, water, shelter), safety, love and belonging, self-esteem or self-respect, and then self-actualization.

[10] http://www.theatlantic.com/business/archive/2012/04/how-america-spends-money-100-years-in-the-life-of-the-family-budget/255475/

[11] http://www.gti.net/mocolib1/prices/2010.html

[12] http://www.mayoclinic.org/tests-procedures/meditation/in-depth/meditation/art-20045858

[13] http://www.sciencedirect.com/science/article/pii/S0022103112000212

[14] Portions of this chapter appeared in *Pittsburgh Catholic Magazine*.

[15] From Investopedia: "A rule stating that in order to find the number of years required to double your money at a given interest rate, you divide the compound return into 72. The result is the approximate number of years that it will take for your investment to double."

[16] Parts of this section adapted from http://isaacmorehouse.com/2013/04/30/1029/

Made in the USA
Charleston, SC
04 January 2016